Breaking into the Biz

The Insider's Guide to Launching
an Entertainment Industry Career

by Jenny Yerrick Martin

Your
IndustryInsider

Breaking in, Moving Up, Making It in Entertainment

COPYRIGHT NOTICE:

LEGAL NOTICE:

This book is dedicated to the industry professionals who have generously shared their stories on YourIndustryInsider.com and to the hundreds of people I have interviewed for jobs, whether they got the job or not. Especially Brian Martin, who definitely got the job.

CONTENTS

PHASE THREE: GETTING IN THE GAME

PROLOGUE

It's the most hated job interview question a young person can hear: "Where do you see yourself in ten years?" Ten years is a long time. Who can possibly have that kind of vision?

Fourteen-year-old Jimmy Fallon had that kind of vision. As a teenager, the future late-night TV host had one goal. When he blew out his birthday candles or saw a shooting star zoom across the sky, he wished to be on *Saturday Night Live*. For years he hung onto that wish, and he would share his aspirations with anyone who asked about them. In fact, as a young man starting out in entertainment, Jimmy was encouraged by someone in the industry to set a broader goal, since the chances of getting on *Saturday Night Live* were one in a million.

BUT JIMMY DIDN'T WANT ANOTHER GOAL. HE WANTED TO BE ON *SNL*.

And in 1999, he was hired on *Saturday Night Live*. Ten years after he had set that one-in-a-million goal, he made it a reality. Here's the thing, though: Jimmy didn't just want to be on *SNL* and then – *poof* – there he was, as if a genie had made it happen. He worked for it. He had a vision of where he wanted to be, and then everything he did in the ensuing years (also known as the rest of his childhood and very early adulthood) was geared toward making it a reality. He honed his impressions, did standup comedy, and studied the successful cast members back to the beginning of the show. This guy was *passionate* and *focused*.

WHAT IT TAKES

You hear similar stories from many of the most successful people in the business – and not just the famous ones. These visions were the gas in the engine that drove them, that made them work hard and overcome obstacles and ignore the many NOs they inevitably heard on the way to the big YESes. And it continues to drive them as they work in their long sought-after careers.

Even if you don't know exactly where in the entertainment industry you want to be in ten years, if you give it some thought, you can already identify some of the key elements. And the more you hone your image of what you want from your professional life and study those who have followed similar paths and seek guidance from those with insider knowledge, the better your odds will be of getting where you want to go. Yes, it takes forethought and effort, but we both know it will be worth it as you make progress and ultimately get to the places you now only dream of being.

THE MYTH VERSUS THE REALITY

There is so much fear, uncertainty, and frustration involved in launching a career in entertainment. The established perception has been created largely through films and television shows depicting the industry, as well as on TMZ and in the celebrity press. The resulting image for outsiders is a mishmash of overnight stardom and affluence, and huge falls from grace resulting in poverty, jail time, and tabloid infamy. But assuming you are not a troubled celebrity or the figment of a particularly creative writer's imagination, that entertainment industry is not your entertainment industry.

The real entertainment industry is a multibillion-dollar business much larger and more functional than you could imagine. Though the hub of the industry is in Los Angeles, with the six major movie studios and the entertainment divisions of the four television networks headquartered here, there are thousands of opportunities throughout the country for those with entertainment aspirations.

A JOB – AND NOT JUST ANY JOB

Yes, I know when you are on the outside, it seems there is a big moat around the industry, or maybe just a wall between you and landing a job – *any* job – in the industry. Trust me. I know. It can be a challenge just to get in.

However, I have been a hiring executive for many years and have had the pleasure of welcoming many newcomers into the industry. And in my one-on-one work with clients, as a professional résumé writer and career consultant, and through group programs and speaking engagements, I have helped many more. So for you, reading this right now… Help has arrived!

Whether you are in Los Angeles or not, a recent grad or a not-so-recent grad (or even someone still in school wanting to make the right moves early on), this book will walk you through the process of identifying and landing that all-important first job.

I will pull back the curtain and give you insight from the true inside, from my experience and extensive research, interviewing and studying hundreds of people who have broken in and achieved their goals, or found unexpected places of career satisfaction and success.

As Chinese philosopher Lao-Tzu said, "The journey of 1,000 miles starts with a single step." We've got a lot of ground to cover, so let's get moving.

But first a bit about me …

MY STORY

When I graduated from Boston University's College of Communications, I'll admit I didn't exactly have a plan to conquer the industry.

Oh sure, I had hopes and dreams, but as to how to get from the diploma grab at Nickerson Field to being a working member of the industry? Nada.

I actually never intended to move to Los Angeles. When I graduated from college, I was very clear that L.A. was alien territory, populated with "not my people." I pictured a population ripped from the pages of supermarket tabloids and, well, I didn't even know what to think might lurk on the *business* side of the business. A bunch of fast-talking plastic-surgeried maniacs, perhaps? Yes, I wanted to be in the business, but I didn't want it to be *that* business, whatever that meant.

So after a very brief post-graduate stay in my native Bethesda, Maryland, I headed to Minneapolis with nothing in particular in mind other than that it seemed to be a cool place. And, in what I then considered a lucky break, I ended up in the movie business there.

Yes, it was lucky that I landed by chance in a town with a small but healthy production community and in a circle of new friends with entertainment connections, but I got into it because I did the legwork, pursued the leads, and demonstrated the passion, commitment, and work ethic to get hired twice and then to get an even bigger opportunity – a bigger opportunity with a catch, though.

Despite my misgivings, I had visited Los Angeles early in my Minneapolis film career, staying with some of the people I met on the first movie I had worked on. And though I liked these people, I disliked L.A. tremendously. Not in the way I had disliked it when my opinion was based on movie and television depictions of the city, but still, that trip created in me a firm commitment to keep my distance.

After I'd worked on two movies in the Twin Cities as a Production Assistant making peanuts (which was okay, because it cost peanuts to live in

Minneapolis), I got a call from the Property Master on the first movie I had worked on. She was looking for an assistant for her next project, a movie that was shooting in – you guessed it – L.A. I would be going from my usual sub-entry-level wages to making $700 a week, and someone else in Los Angeles was offering me a free place to stay.

What could I do? I put all my worldly belongings in storage and vowed to return to Minneapolis in six months. Which I did. I returned to get my worldly belongings out of storage and drive them to L.A. in a rickety van co-piloted by my friend Lou, who would herself relocate to L.A. a few years later. Eventually Lou became the costume designer on Ryan Murphy's series *Popular*, then *Nip/Tuck*, then *Glee*, then *American Horror Story*. (See Lou's profile on Your Industry Insider for more information on her path: http://yourindustryinsider.com/2010/09/loueyrich/.)

Fast-forward over twenty years, and I am still in Los Angeles and still in the business. I stopped hating the city about a year and a half into my time here. And once I had been working in the business a decent amount of time, I realized that though there are some plastic-surgeried maniacs (and a fair amount of Ari Golds and Ari Gold wannabes, in case you *Entourage* fans were wondering), the entertainment industry is a large and diverse community mainly comprising smart, dedicated, insanely hard-working individuals.

After a couple years as a prop assistant, I quit freelance crew work because I wanted more stability and time for my own creative projects. I worked outside the business for a couple of years, and then got back in through temping at many different entertainment companies.

One of the companies I temped at was a studio-based film production company. I was the temporary receptionist/mailroom person until I was hired after a few weeks to be the permanent receptionist/mailroom person. From there I worked a few jobs in that company over the years, eventually working my way into the position responsible for hiring, among other things. At one point, I hired the man who would become my husband. (Yes, I'm *that* good at hiring.)

Over the course of my years as an entertainment industry hiring executive, I have interviewed more than 1,000 job candidates. Many of them were just out of college, where a textbook and a knowledgeable professor had guided them through every subject they wanted to learn about. Now they were trying to get into the industry, but they didn't know how the job I was trying to fill would help them get where they wanted to go in the industry.

In a lot of cases, they wanted to be in television or music, or maybe they wanted to work on a film set. I was interviewing them for a job in the offices of a film production company. The position I was filling would get them into the entertainment industry, sure, but in the completely wrong part of it for what they wanted to do. As a hiring executive, I definitely didn't want to have them figure that out right after I hired them and then pursue a more appropriate job, leaving me to fill the position again.

Luckily, I found I liked talking with people about the industry – how it works, who does what, how to get from point A to point B to whatever destination inside the industry the person was interested in. As they often told me, our brief interview gave these job candidates more insider knowledge about how the business works than any resource they'd ever had before. Clearly they needed more than a finger pointing them in the right direction.

Creating a website to share this knowledge, YourIndustryInsider.com, was a natural next step for me. In addition to sharing my experience and expert advice, I have profiled or shared guest posts from more than 100 members of the entertainment industry within L.A. and scattered all over the country. I love hearing their stories, identifying the common ground that has helped them become successful and the unique strategies and tactics they used to get where they wanted to go.

As a student of the industry, I love telling real-world stories of what works and what doesn't work, as well as creative ways to get into the biz, to transition from one area to another within it, and to make leaps up the ladder to new career levels. It's hugely gratifying to provide a real-life picture of such a misunderstood industry.

The successful entertainment professionals I profile for Your Industry Insider often say they wish they'd had the site when they were starting out. I wish I'd had it, too!

HOW TO USE THIS BOOK

This book is a comprehensive step-by-step guide to identifying and landing your first job, as well as setting yourself up for a long and fruitful entertainment industry career.

Phase One, "Career Planning," will help you figure out what you want from the industry and how to make money while pursuing your dream or start out the right way to reach a particular position in the industry.

Phase Two, "Readying Your Resources," is about customizing your job hunt materials (résumés, cover letters) as well as your online identity (LinkedIn, Facebook, Twitter, blogging) to market you for the position or area of the industry you identified as your target in Part One.

Phase Three, "Getting in the Game," will walk you through actually breaking into the business. You'll move forward with the tools you created in Part Two to find opportunities and assess them, submit yourself for consideration to those opportunities that seem to be a good fit, and ace the interview.

HOWEVER, though it is highly readable, this is not a book you just read. If you simply read it and do not do anything recommended in it, you will not get any closer to starting your career in the industry. You will not be even one step closer to realizing your ambitions in the industry.

The Action Prompts throughout the book are designed to tell you when you need to apply what you are reading to your own path. Checklists at the end of each chapter keep you on track, moving forward, and on your way to being gainfully employed.

Your future career is waiting, and you have before you a roadmap in. Ready to get started?

PHASE ONE: CAREER PLANNING

It all begins with a vision. Whether that vision is as specific as winning an Emmy for Best Costumes or being a regular on a sitcom or creating a video game that takes E3 by storm, or as general as working at a film studio or on a set, it is the all-important first step toward career success and satisfaction. Take a moment to close your eyes and picture yourself working in entertainment. What do you see?

As you go through "Phase One: Career Planning," you will have help discovering and narrowing your entertainment career goals. The work you do here will determine how you shape your job hunt tools, online presence, and pitch in "Phase Two: Readying Your Resources," and how you begin your entertainment career in "Phase Three: Getting in the Game."

{ Reminder: Landing the right job at the end of this process depends on following the Action Prompts and making sure you've checked off all the items on the Section Checklist before you move forward. Do not skip anything unless you are told it doesn't apply to you. }

CHAPTER 1
THE BIG PICTURE

Jay Z knew from a young age that he loved nothing more than creating rhymes and performing them for friends. This was before there was even a market for hip-hop, before the first big single, before the name "hip-hop" (or "rap") had even been given to the musical style. A high school dropout, Jay Z had a lucrative albeit short-lived career as a drug dealer before getting into the fledgling hip-hop scene and making a name for himself. From there, he became a successful performer, producer, record label owner, clothing line mogul, sports team part owner, nightclub co-owner, and sometimes even actor.

Sean John Combs (aka "Diddy") attended Howard University in D.C. He interned at a New York record company and dropped out of college when he was hired there. After a couple of years of developing talent for that company, he founded his own label and produced some of the most popular hip-hop records of the mid-'90s. In 1997, he recorded his first commercial vocal and launched his own career as a performer. From his early beginnings, he has grown his interests to include not only producing records, but owning clothing lines, co-owning restaurants, producing a TV show, acting, and launching a music channel.

The lesson here is that there's more than one way to make it as a hip-hop superstar. Though neither man was aiming for that "title" when starting out, both men's careers started with a passion for music and a vision of what they wanted their lives to look like, and grew from there. In Jay Z's case, performing was the way in. For Diddy, it was identifying and developing talent in others. And though Jay Z's "day job" while he pursued his passion was drug dealing, you'll note that neither he nor Diddy strayed from the music end of the business. Diddy even managed to get himself the right internship while in college, an internship that led him to the job that gave him his start.

As Jay Z and Diddy have discussed in many interviews (and as Jay Z details in his book Decoded), each of them worked extremely hard, took advantage of opportunities, came back from failure, studied and learned from other people's mistakes and triumphs, networked and developed relationships, found mentors and listened to their guidance, and made a series of large and small strategic moves designed to get them where they wanted to go.

This is not just something you see in famous entertainment industry figures. Thousands of people have successful entertainment careers in Los Angeles, New York, and around the country. You'll notice the professionals profiled on my entertainment career site, YourIndustryInsider.com, either knew early on exactly what they wanted to do or, more frequently, explored their interests in the industry and eventually had a "this is it" moment. From there, a vision developed that informed their work, their trajectory, and their determination.

For Mike Knobloch, now President of Film Music and Publishing at Universal Pictures, a visit to a scoring stage while working as a Production Assistant on the movie *Father of the Bride* set the course for the rest of his career. He recognized that the intersection of music and movies was where he wanted to work. How to get there didn't immediately become clear, but when it did, he headed in that direction and was not deterred. He now has a top job in film music, one of only six people working at that level in the entire industry.

Antoine Sanfuentes, who is Senior Vice President, NBC News, and formerly the NBC News Washington Bureau Chief, came to the organization as an intern while studying anthropology at American University. In order to take an internship at the NBC Washington bureau and get credit for it, he had to convince his advisor that working in the news division was relevant to his major. At the time, it seemed like a stretch, but the passion for studying humanity coupled with having enjoyed countless family dinner table conversations about current events perfectly prepared him for a career covering U.S. politics. It's not surprising he has thrived and ended up in a top job there.

Your ability to create a successful and satisfying career starts with a vision, too. Maybe you don't have a one-in-a-million target, like Jimmy Fallon did with wanting to be on *Saturday Night Live*. Maybe you don't even have a consuming passion, like Jay Z and Sean "Diddy" Combs did with music. But there is something that fuels you to be in the industry, and the more clearly you can identify what that fuel is and use it to lead you, to inspire and inform all the decisions you make as you move forward, the better your chances are of maintaining a fulfilling career in entertainment.

ACTION PROMPT 1

This is a warm-up exercise to get you thinking creatively and really plugging in to YOU, and what turns you on and makes YOU happy (not, I repeat, NOT thinking about every piece of career advice you've ever gotten from friends, family, and others). This should be a fun, creative process – not a dull, stressful process. So...

Either crack open a fresh notebook or start a new document on your computer for the "thought work you will be doing (everything that is not creating a job hunt–related document, such as a résumé, a tracking worksheet, etc).

In no particular order and with no particular format, answer these questions:

WHAT DO YOU LOVE DOING?

WHAT DO YOU LOVE READING/WATCHING/LISTENING TO?

WHAT ARE YOUR FAVORITE WEBSITES?

WHERE DO YOU LOVE TO GO?

WHO WOULD YOU LOVE TO MEET?

WHAT TOPICS INTEREST YOU MOST?

This is a brain dump. Don't censor yourself and don't try to link the items; just write whatever comes into your head.

EXAMPLE – My page might look like this:

Field of Dreams, the books of Martha Beck, self-actualization, historical fiction, biographies of successful people, Richard Branson, Tina Fey, Parks & Recreation, museums, Deadline Hollywood, Steve Carell, The Mindy Project, Europe, Fresh Air, This American Life, Facebook...

CHAPTER 2
THE "WHAT," THE "WHY,"
AND PRACTICAL CONSIDERATIONS

Lady Gaga wouldn't be happy with Taylor Swift's career. And Tom Cruise wouldn't be happy with Johnny Depp's career. Why not? In the case of the first two, they're both singers, right? And Cruise and Depp are highly successful actors. So why couldn't you just switch their career choices, their songs, and their screen credits respectively and have them be equally satisfied?

Well, if you've listened to interviews with any of them, you know a little about what inspires and motivates them. For Lady Gaga, an integral part of her perfor-mance (and not just while she is on stage) is being provocative, using the way she dresses to make a statement and sometimes even make people uncom-fortable. Taylor Swift wants to use the music itself to express her personal journey and move people emotionally. I think we can be pretty sure Taylor Swift wouldn't put on Lady Gaga's "meat dress" to go to an event any more than Lady Gaga would be so nakedly confessional in her songwriting.

Tom Cruise likes to challenge himself physically and has preferred to remain in "classic action star" roles for the most part, with an occasional foray into main-stream comedy. Throughout his career, Johnny Depp has chosen to play quirky characters in smaller movies (up until some recent blockbuster titles). He has been a frequent collaborator with director Tim Burton, appearing in many of his films. Based on the career choices they have made, we can assume Cruise wouldn't have wanted to play cross-dressing B-film director Ed Wood any more than Depp would want to be the star of the *Mission Impossible* franchise.

As you might have gleaned from the above, there are two main components that make up a career path. There is the "what," which is the target job itself; there is the "why," the motivation behind it. There is also a third component that takes into account the life beyond the job, the practical considerations.

ACTION PROMPT 2

Determine your "what," your "why," & practical considerations.

Before you move on, I want you to revisit the brain dump you did for Action Prompt 1; so if you skipped it or half-assed it, go back and work on it now. It's important. We'll wait.

Okay, let's look at my brain dump example first:
Field of Dreams, the books of Martha Beck, self-actualization, historical fiction, biographies of successful people, Richard Branson, Tina Fey, Parks & Recreation, museums, Deadline Hollywood, Steve Carell, The Mindy Project, Europe, Fresh Air, This American Life, Facebook...

In the following three through lines of my brain dump, you can see the seeds for what my career is now:
1. **Love of storytelling** – I write and make others write compelling résumés and other job hunt materials and, on Your Industry Insider, profile accomplished entertainment professionals.
2. **Love of entertainment** – both the end products and the behind-the-scenes stories; I study and share insider insights on having successful entertainment careers.
3. **Interest in self-actualization** – I help people conceptualize and have successful, fulfilling careers.

You get the idea. Now reread your brain dump (and add to it any time you think of another answer to one of the questions) and keep it in mind as you move forward.

Step One: Define Your "What"
Your "what" is simply the current answer to the question "What do you want to be when you grow up?" or "What do you want to be now?" if you are all grown up and have already entered the professional world.

Your "what" might be a specific position, such as a singer, an actor, a marketing executive, a composer, or a talent agent, or it might more general, such as TV production crew member or entertainment executive.

⭐ Write down as much as you know of your "what." If you don't have one, use "entertainment professional" as a placeholder.

Step Two: Examine Your "Why"

When you close your eyes and envision yourself working in television or film or as a marketing executive or a composer, what do you picture? Think about being really happy working, loving what you do. What do you see? Do you picture having a nice house? Do you see your name mentioned in articles? Leading a team in an important meeting? Working in the middle of the night on a set?

⭐ **Write down the answer to these questions to get into your "why":**

Is it important for you to be famous? If so, how famous? Well-known in your community/niche? Within your field? Or world-famous?

Is it important for you to move people emotionally with your work?

Is it important for you to make gangster money or just enough to be comfortable?

Is it important for you to lead an organization? Your own organization or an existing one?

Is it important for you to be part of a team, to collaborate on projects? Are you more comfortable in a creative environment or within a more corporate organization?

Do you like a "ladder" to climb (an established path to your desired position) or do you prefer a situation where you have to chart your own course?

Step Three: Identify Your Practical Considerations

In addition to the motivations behind your chosen position or field, there are the other factors beyond what you actually do for a living that have to do with what your life needs to look like so that you feel content each day.

Write down the answers to these questions (and any other practical considerations you have that are not presented below):

Is it important for you to have stability (i.e., a consistent job that provides benefits)?

Is it important for you to travel a lot? To not travel at all?

Is it important for you to stay in an office and work steady hours?

Do you need to work only certain hours (daytime, nighttime, weekdays, weekends) to leave other time free for pursuing a dream job, caring for a young child, or something else?

How do you feel about living in Los Angeles versus living elsewhere? Do you have a specific place or type of place in mind?

How do you feel about commuting? Is there a certain distance you would be willing to drive each day to get to a job? (This is a key Los Angeles question.)

Do you prefer to work really hard for certain stretches of time and then take time off?

Would you be willing to get an additional degree, certification, or training to pursue the right position?

To illustrate how this all adds up to a fulfilling career path and satisfying life beyond it, here are some examples of industry professionals and their answers to the above questions:

ALISON

Alison wants to work in television but doesn't know what position she wants. Ultimately she would like to lead an organization, though not necessarily her own. She likes working as part of a team, and having a ladder to climb appeals to her. Stability is a priority, both in having a steady paycheck and maintaining a consistent work schedule. She does not mind school and is happy to move wherever necessary in order to have the right opportunity.

Alison could go to law school and end up as a talent agent in the TV department of a major agency. She could also be a business affairs executive at a TV network, cable channel, or studio. If she chose not to go to law school, she could work in programming or one of the other departments at a network, cable channel, TV studio, or production company. Ultimately, she could be the head of her department or even end up as CEO of the organization she is in.

JEFF

Jeff wants to be a composer. He wants to create scores for either TV shows or movies or both. Beyond that, he wants to be known in his niche and well off, but he has no interest in fame or in what it would take to earn gangster money. He likes the idea of working as part of a team and must be in a creative environment in order to do his job well. He enjoys traveling, up to a point. Stability is not a consideration for him, but he needs to stay close to the New York City area, where his elderly parents live. He already has a degree in composition from a prestigious music school and studies on his own to further his skill set.

Jeff has a pretty clear path in mind. He needs to take advantage of the opportunities that exist for composers in New York as well as reach out to establish contacts in Los Angeles, if he can, since traveling there for short periods is an option for him. He should probably try to focus on TV work, since the pace and format demands more rapid collaboration and teamwork, and film composing can be solitary for long stretches.

Networking with musicians, engineers, postproduction pros, and others who might know of opportunities or be in a position to hire him is key. He should also make sure his demos are top-notch. Jeff's will be a career path he'll make up as he goes along, and it will be important for him to have a compatible day job or complementary career that will allow him the flexibility to take scoring jobs when they come up.

You can see by the above examples that even without a "what," you can still get plenty of clues from your "why" and from how you envision the rest of your life. In Alison's case, she had no specific position she was aiming for, but by identifying what motivated her and what was important to her, she could lay out a path for herself that was likely to lead to long-term success and personal satisfaction. Jeff had a target position, and his plan was all about setting up the right life around it and strategizing about how to break in and build a career path.

You might be wondering when you'll actually "make it" in the biz. Let's move on to that topic.

CHAPTER 3
THE LOS ANGELES QUESTION (AKA THE "WHERE" OF YOUR CAREER)

"Do you have to live in Los Angeles in order to have a successful entertainment career in your chosen position?"

It's a question many recent grads and others with showbiz aspirations agonize over. In some cases, the answer is obvious. If you want to work for one of the major studios, the entertainment divisions of any of the TV networks, or the top talent agencies, L.A. is a must.

However, there are versions of the other organizations that make up the industry scattered across the country (and in countries around the world). There are film and television crews, production companies, and post houses. There are record labels, recording studios, music publishers, and, of course, musical performers. And there are representatives (agents, managers, publicists, and entertainment lawyers) wherever there are people who need representation for their entertainment careers. In other words, just about everywhere.

"What are the Advantages and Disadvantages to Launching Your Entertainment Career Somewhere Other than Los Angeles?"

I actually believe all young actors should spend some time in an urban environment which is not L.A., doing theater, getting their feet wet, and living the life of a growing artist. It's hard to do that in L.A. L.A. is a pretty disconnected place where people have to find their community, or create a community. I see young actors come here all the time and feel isolated. If you can start somewhere else, that's great.

Risa Bramon Garcia, Director/Casting Director/Acting Teacher, on YourIndustryInsider.com

Risa actually has something there. Starting outside L.A. sounds appealingly low-risk. You dip your toes in the entertainment water, maybe even while still living at home with your folks. But then you fear you will miss out if you wait to move, that moving at the beginning of your career might be easier in some ways, or that it will be harder to make a lateral move into L.A. when all of your experience is elsewhere.

PROS OF MOVING TO L.A. WITH NO EXPERIENCE

★ There are a lot of opportunities and structures in place in which to get in and move up in certain parts of the industry. You can follow a path that other people have successfully traveled to get in and move up.

★ You can start to know who's who and even make contact with some of those people in power and begin to climb the right ladder, if your goals involve a ladder.

★ You are joining a large pool of people without entertainment experience to network and socialize with as you all struggle to break in. Those people will become your "class" in the same way that you worked your way through high school and college with the same people.

★ When you do start to establish yourself, you will be making a name for yourself in a place where there is no limit. You can aim to become the head of a major studio, a blockbuster producer, or the top talent manager in the business knowing that you are getting degrees closer to your big goal with each step you take, each person you meet.

PROS OF LAUNCHING WHERE YOU ARE

★ You can test-drive your dreams without uprooting yourself and moving away from family, friends, and safety net.

★ You won't be a tiny fish in a huge pond if you pick a smaller city to launch from. (You might be a tiny fish in a pretty big pond depending upon where you live, but it's still probably much less intimidating.)

★ You won't risk losing focus on your larger pursuits in the struggle to find a good job and pay the rent. (NOTE: The cost of living is considerably higher in L.A. than most other places in the U.S. – but almost a bargain compared to Boston, San Francisco, and NYC.)

★ If you are a creative, you can concentrate on creating great samples of your work to show around (i.e., scripts if you are an aspiring writer, content for your reel if you are an aspiring actor, director, director of photography, etc.) or getting relevant experience for your résumé without the distraction of relocation and all it entails.

★ Being outside the epicenter of the industry gives you the creative freedom to not just think outside the box, but to not even know what "the box" is, with "the box" being current conventional wisdom about what is "good" or "trendy." You could create something really fresh by being in your own corner of the world, not mixed in with a lot of people trying to do the same thing you are doing.

THE BOTTOM-LINE QUESTION: "IS LOS ANGELES RIGHT FOR YOU?"

No matter what phase of your career you are in, there are a lot of considerations behind the L.A. question: financial, logistical, emotional, professional.

Maybe your parents and siblings are somewhere else and it's important to be close to them. Maybe you have a family of your own and hate to uproot them.

Maybe you hate the gloomy weather where you are now and know L.A. weather would give your quality of life a bump.

Maybe you see that the cost of living in the other city you are considering is much lower and you know that when you are just starting out, that can make a big difference on your life.

You *know* your entertainment job prospects are better in Los Angeles than anywhere else strictly because of the amount of opportunities there.

How are you supposed to untangle this web of considerations and make a good decision about such an important matter?

There is a tool I discovered not long ago, and I wish I had it when I was starting out and had to wing all sorts of forks in my career path (and personal life, for that matter).

It is called the Weighted Average Decision Matrix (WADM), and it helps you quantify all the various factors and make as objective a decision as you possibly can by assigning numerical values to each element in your decision and rating each of those elements for your different options.

Example: Let's say you are trying to decide between Los Angeles, Austin, and San Francisco. Your family is in Northern California and you love the lifestyle in Austin (based on visiting a friend there several times), but you really want to work in television.

You make four columns, the one on the left for each factor in your decision and the other three for the different cities you are considering, like this:

| Location Factors | Los Angeles | Austin | San Francisco |

Then you list each of the factors and give them a numerical value (1-10) based on how important they are to your decision, with 10 being of top importance. Place the value in parentheses next to the Location Factor. In the example below, cost of living rates 6 in terms of importance, and career opportunities rates 9. Go ahead and give your own ratings (you can repeat number ratings):

Location Factors	Los Angeles	Austin	San Francisco
Cost of Living (6)			
Proximity to Family (6)			
Weather (4)			
Career Opportunities (9)			
Ease of meeting people/ Social scene (7)			

Now, rate each city by placing a numerical value for each factor in that city's column, again rating 1-10 where 10 is the highest value:

Location Factors	Los Angeles	Austin	San Francisco
Cost of Living (6)	8	4	8
Proximity to Family (6)	7	4	10
Weather (4)	10	8	6
Career Opportunities (9)	10	6	4
Ease of meeting people/ Social scene (7)	4	10	8

Next, multiply the number in parenthesis from the Location Factors column by its rating in the city column, and enter that total back in the city column. Finally, add up each column for a total score for each city:

Location Factors	Los Angeles	Austin	San Francisco
Cost of Living (6)	48	24	48
Proximity to Family (6)	42	24	60
Weather (4)	40	32	24
Career Opportunities (9)	90	54	36
Ease of meeting people/ Social scene (7)	28	70	56
	248	204	224

In this example, the WADM of 248 would indicate the person would move to Los Angeles, with San Francisco and Austin ranked at 224 and 204 respectively. But if they added another couple of factors or rethought how they weighted them, the WADM totals might shift into San Francisco's favor.

It's not an exact science and at some point, the "gut feeling" might take over this decision, but if the gut is confused, this is an excellent tool. And if you don't want to do the math by hand, there's a website called helpmydecision.com that will do the math for you.

 ACTION PROMPT 3

If you already know where you are going to be for this phase of your career, congratulations. You can skip this section.
Otherwise, it's time to examine your options:
★ What cities are you seriously considering living in?
★ What factors are affecting your decision?

Write the answers to these two questions in the notebook or computer document where you put the "brain dump" from Action Prompt 1 and the answers to the "Your 'What,' Your 'Why,' & Practical Considerations" questions from Action Prompt 2.

You don't have to use the WADM if you already have a clear idea after considering the options and the factors weighing your decision or talking them over with a trusted friend or advisor.

But if you need a little help making the decision, it can't hurt to try the WADM. Nobody will hold you to the results if you decide they don't make sense for you, but you may just end up with a clear-cut answer.

Here is a summary of the instructions, but refer to the above example as needed:
★ Make a column for your Location Factors along the left side and then as many other columns as cities you are deciding between.
★ Write your factors along the left side and your potential locations along the top.
★ Give each factor a number representing how important it is in this decision and then rate each city for that factor.
★ Multiply the importance rating for the factor by the rating for each city to determine the ranking for each city in that category.
★ Add up each column to see how each city fares for these factors.

If one city does not have a considerably higher number than the others, you might need to add other factors to help with the decision, or call that trusted friend again to go over your quandary.

CHAPTER 4
THE PATH TO WHERE
YOU WANT TO GO

You have your "brain dump" of breadcrumb clues from the first Action Prompt. You have your "what" or at least a reasonable idea of "why" and your list of practical considerations. You know your "where" – that is, *where* you are going to start your entertainment career. How does it all add up to getting the right job on your path to where you want to go?

That's a good question, and one I've faced many times consulting with recent grads and others with entertainment ambitions, and as a hiring executive interviewing candidates for an entry-level job. Whether they have a very specific idea of where they want to go in the industry or they have only an inkling of what they want their career to look like, many are at a loss about how to identify a path and how to determine the best first step on that path.

In other words, what job should they be looking for now and how do they move forward from that job toward the goal that for them will mean "making it" in the industry?

Wow. Sounds like something you're going to have to guess at and then hope for the best, right?

You know better than that. And as a former college student (or maybe even a current student), you know how to get information. It's called a research project, and it's time to get to it.

There are three sources for this research project: Internet searches, firsthand sources, and firsthand experience.

INTERNET RESEARCH (PLUS BOOKS AND OTHER CONTENT ABOUT YOUR FIELD)

The Internet is chock-full of stories of successful entertainment professionals whose paths can educate you on possible entry points for your own career. Of course, start on YourIndustryInsider.com. Besides there, you can go to professional organizations for people in the field you are aspiring to, such as

The Writer's Guild, Director's Guild, Producer's Guild, Costume Designer's Guild, etc. They usually have profiles of successful members on their site or on the online version of an affiliated publication.

If sites that feature a specific position or field aren't right for your search, try doing a Google search for the name of the position or field you are interested in, such as "film development executive" or "TV network programming executive." Also, look on LinkedIn for employees at the type of organization they would work at; for example, do a company search for Sony Pictures and look for positions that interest you. This will probably turn up only first-, second-, or third-degree connections depending upon your membership level on LinkedIn, so it might not work – but it's worth a shot.

You can also Google the names of people you know of who have entertainment jobs you are interested in finding out about. If you watch a movie or TV show and are particularly impressed by some aspect of it, such as the writing or the production design, look on IMDB.com (Internet Movie Database) to find out the name of the writer or production designer, then search for more information about that person by name.

While you are doing your Internet research, consider broadening your search terms to find out about alternative opportunities to apply your passions and experience. For instance, if you think you want to be a film producer, search for "commercial producer," "TV producer," "promo producer," "web series producer," "reality TV producer," and/or "transmedia producer." This research may turn up an even more fitting path for you than the biggies everyone tries to pursue.

One example of someone who found her niche in an alternative to producing films is Michelle Jackino, who was profiled on YourIndustryInsider.com in 2011. She is now the Executive Creative Director of top promo house The Ant Farm. She didn't have a clear direction when she started in entertainment, just a for film. Through her internship experience and her first couple of jobs, she realized she didn't have the patience for long form and that promo producing was a great match for her. She is at the top of her field, and has worked with filmmakers such as Clint Eastwood and Martin Scorsese creating trailers for their work and won many awards over the years. How's that for a good fit for a film lover?

Also, find books about the field you are interested in, and watch TV shows and documentaries that cover them, too. For instance, New York Times Media Reporter Bill Carter has written books covering the machinations behind two famous late-night television transitions. The first, *The Late Shift*, covers when Johnny Carson retired from *The Tonight Show* and Jay Leno and David Letterman vied to take over as host. The second, *The War for Late Night*, details the more recent transition: Jay Leno was forced out to make way for Conan O'Brien as host of *The Tonight Show*, but O'Brien was subsequently ousted in favor of the reinstallation of Leno. Even if you aren't interested in late-night television, you can learn a lot about the television field by reading those.

Another great book about TV is *Top of the Rock: Inside the Rise and Fall of Must-See TV* by former NBC entertainment chief Warren Littlefield. And if you want to get an inside scoop on the film business, two books by producer Lynda Obst are must-reads. *Hello, He Lied, and Other Tales from the Hollywood Trenches* is a great recent history but a little dated, published in 1997. *Sleepless in Hollywood: Tales from the New Abnormal in the Movie Business* is a current portrait of the film industry from the true inside and will give you pause about joining it.

There are plenty of other books, TV shows, and documentaries about the entertainment industry, so include finding the right ones for you while you are doing your Internet research.

FIRSTHAND SOURCES

Arguably a better source than Internet research is finding someone you can talk with directly about a given path. You can ask questions and may get insider tips that aren't included in the articles you read on the Internet. I recommend doing some Internet research on a given path before you reach out to talk one-on-one with someone about that path, because the more you know, the better your questions will be. So if there is a position or an area of the industry you are interested in finding out more about, do your research. Then see if you can work your network to find someone in that position for a quick Q&A.

You may be able to reach these people through someone you know (your professors, peers, existing industry contacts) or people you may be connected to through social media. Even people on Twitter can be very receptive if you take the time to interact and build a rapport. Commenting on and retweeting their content, complimenting them on their work when applicable, and asking questions are good ways to connect.

FIRSTHAND EXPERIENCE

The third source of information about what you think you want to do – and arguably the most important – is to actually try it out. You want to be a music manager, an entertainment marketing executive, a producer? Have you done this outside your school projects? If not, how do you know you'd be good at it in the real world, or that you'd like doing it without the support of an academic environment? You really don't know.

Find an unrepresented band and try to get gigs for them and build their following. Approach someone with an entertainment product (YouTube program, website, etc) and offer to market it. Produce a web short. It goes without saying that if you want to be a writer you should write a bunch of whatever it is you want to write professionally (TV sitcom or drama scripts, screenplays, etc.). But regardless of what the desired career is, there are all sorts of opportunities to try out a given career in the entertainment industry. Choose one and find out if it's really for you.

Plus, if you want to do something creative, what I call a "dream job," you have to create it yourself before anyone is going to hire you. That's right: Nobody is going to pay you to write the script for something or direct something or com-pose the soundtrack for something or act in something unless you have proven you can do it. There is nothing you can have on your résumé that will get you hired as a film producer except related experience. Even if you did not get paid, producing a film and getting it seen on the festival circuit – or better yet, bought for distribution – is the only way you can prove yourself as a producer.

Yes, it takes a lot of hustle to produce an indie film – but it takes a lot of hustle to produce a big-budget studio film, too, so if you don't love it, being a film producer is not for you. Luckily, there are thousands of jobs in the industry to choose from, so you won't be at a loss for alternatives.

Let's use young Jimmy Fallon as an example for this section. You'll recall that from the time he was 14, he wanted to be on *Saturday Night Live*. So he studied all of the early cast members. He knew who could do celebrity impressions and who sang, who played wacky characters, who was a writer in addition to being a performer and what they wrote, and the background of each of the "Not Ready for Primetime" Players, as they were called back in the early days of the show. That knowledge guided him as he pursued his dreams.

He probably would've talked with people who worked on the show firsthand when he was still a teenager (Who knows? Maybe he sent fan letters to cast members or even creator/producer Lorne Michaels), but you can bet that as he grew up, he talked with anyone he knew about his dream. In fact, it was one of the teachers at the famed improvisational and sketch comedy troupe and school, The Groundlings, who told him he should set a broader goal. She didn't realize how laser-focused he was. (Jimmy Fallon's name is now listed among the many Groundlings alumni who have gone on to SNL.)

He didn't just test-drive his dream. Following the example of the many *SNL* cast members he had studied, he learned to play guitar and wrote comic songs, did standup, studied sketch comedy and improv (see The Groundlings above), and honed his impressions obsessively.

Jimmy was committed. And if you watch any footage of him on *Saturday Night Live* or on late-night TV, you can see it paid off.

 # ACTION PROMPT 4

Do your own research project.

It's your turn to apply what you've learned above about the three resources for information about your possible career paths. Get out your notebook or open your computer file.

Look on the Internet, read books, watch TV shows and documentaries. Start with YourIndustryInsider.com just to give you an easy jumping-off point with profiles of entertainment professionals and then branch out to sites dedicated to what you want to do/think you want to do. After that, do Google searches with job titles, descriptions of positions, and relevant key words and use the names of people who are actually doing what you aspire to do. Be both focused and open to alternatives. Take detailed notes while doing your research. You never know when you are going to want to come back to something you read about that didn't seem relevant at the time, but later seems promising to investigate.

Talk with people directly.
Use your personal network and social media network to reach out to
people who can help you with your research. Be concise and spell out
why you want to talk to them and what exactly you are asking of them.
Do not ask for a job or be open-ended about what they are agreeing to.

Example: I am a recent grad from Columbia College in Chicago, and
I am interested in possibly pursuing a job in TV programming. I have a
few questions about your career path and would love to sit down with
you (or have a phone call with you) for 10-15 minutes at your convenience
to get some insight on your path and your position. I promise I won't take
up any more of your time. I am just looking for some information.

This email identifies you, asks for a specific type of meeting, and reassures
them that you aren't going to take up a lot of time and that you aren't
going to ask them for a job. Yes, if they like you, they may ask for your
résumé or put you in touch with HR, assuming you are in a position to
be looking for a job, but you don't want to ask for a job or help finding
a job in an informational interview. It is a faux pas and might hurt your
chances of getting help from them or being able to use them as a
resource in the future.

Test-drive your ambition.
This is the most challenging and the most valuable of the items in this
Action Prompt. Nothing beats firsthand experience, both in giving you
a real idea of what a job path is like and in proving you can do it. Of
course there are jobs you cannot test-drive, such as the TV Programming
Executive, which is when reading books about the television business and
having informational interviews comes in handy. But otherwise, find a way
to do the position you aspire to as a side project. Even if you hate doing
it – actually, especially if you hate doing it – you will be glad you gave
it a shot and saved yourself time and energy before you pursued it as
a career.

CHAPTER 5
THE MYTH OF OVERNIGHT SUCCESS

When I was in my mid-twenties, an American Film Institute Writing Program graduate told me that the students are told that it will take an average of ten years for them to break into writing professionally for film and TV, to get their first paid writing gig or first script sale.

That seemed like an incredibly long period of time then, and I dismissed the advice as something a school would tell you if it wanted to temper your expectations. But having interviewed many writers for YourIndustryInsider.com and knowing many personally and professionally, I can now say that it's a fairly accurate estimate.

This chapter applies to all of those who have big entertainment aspirations – screenwriters, songwriters, TV writers, actors, musicians, singers, directors, producers in all fields – positions that for the most part have no "ladder" (progression of positions leading to the top) and require a great deal of hard work and a little luck, or a lot of it, to succeed.

I know this chapter might seem like a splash of cold water on all your dreams of "making it" and you will be tempted to skip it or maybe even throw this book into the nearest garbage can, but don't. The aim here is not to dissuade you from pursuing your dreams, but to prepare you to survive the long haul and know what you're likely to encounter along the way. The old saying "Ignorance is bliss" may be catchy, but ignorance doesn't set you up to survive the lean years, which will no doubt involve perseverance, recovery from setbacks, course correction, and lots and lots of "no"s before and between significant "yes"es.

One of the few true overnight success stories I know of for writers is Josh Schwartz, creator of The O.C., Gossip Girl, and Chuck. He grew up in Providence, Rhode Island with parents who were not connected to the entertainment industry. While attending the University of Southern California, he sold a feature film script and a TV pilot and then dropped out to write full time. When The O.C. went on the air, he became the youngest person to ever create a network series and run it day-to-day. He was 26.

In his book *Outliers*, Malcolm Gladwell talks about how it takes 10,000 hours of doing something to truly become proficient at it. The entertainment example he gives is the legendary rock band The Beatles. When The Beatles were just starting out, they were hired to appear at a Hamburg, Germany club where bands had to play four to eight hours a night seven nights a week. They did this gig for months. "They were no good onstage when they went there and they were very good when they came back," Gladwell quotes Beatles biographer Philip Norman as saying.

Yes, they got good at playing their instruments and at playing together. But they also honed their sound, found out what the crowd reacted to most, and grew their set list. Though there's no doubt it was grueling and on some nights some of them just weren't feeling it, it was an invaluable experience. It was a job. It made them professionals. It gave them confidence.

Josh Schwartz apparently had dreams of being a writer and being in entertainment from a young age. He was a movie lover by all accounts, and he is said to have had a subscription to entertainment trade magazine *Variety* from the age of 12. So even though he made his first sale in college, he was a dedicated student of the industry well before he sold the script.

Another early success story, writer/director/producer J.J. Abrams (*Felicity, Alias, Lost, Mission Impossible 3, Star Trek*), who sold his first film treatment while in college, has said in interviews that he spent countless hours making short films during his childhood, just as his idol Steven Spielberg had done when he was a kid.

So the lesson here is that those who broke through at a young age may have been working hard since a *very* young age. Of course, it doesn't feel like work when you're a kid and you're doing something you love to do. Without a day job or any of the other pressures of adulthood, it's easy to lose yourself in a task or a project and not even give time a second thought.

But the ones who hadn't done the work and still broke in as kids usually either had a lottery-odds lucky break (walking in at *exactly* the right time for the exact right project) or they had family in the business. Yes, Jaden and Willow Smith are a popular example of this phenomenon, but Jake and Maggie Gyllenhaal, Gwyneth Paltrow, and Miley Cyrus also benefited from the access their industry parents could provide.

Even J.J. Abrams had connections. His father was a television producer, and he grew up in an affluent Los Angeles neighborhood. Not to take anything away from these talented and hard-working people, but they did have help with their initial entries into the business, not just through their parents' connections, but also growing up with the offspring of other entertainment pros. At their preschool playdates, these future household names were networking.

So how does someone who grew up in the real world break into the business doing something so many people dream of from the time of playing dress-up in their parents' basement as kids? What does it take to bash through the imaginary and not-so-imaginary walls that keep you from cashing a paycheck while doing what you love to do?

Here are some strategies, actions, and words-to-the-wise to help you on your path:

YOU WILL HAVE TO PUT YOURSELF OUT THERE.

Though you might want to wait until you are "ready" to start networking (by whatever definition you have of "ready"), it's best to get out there while you are honing your craft and developing samples of your work. Start connecting with your peers and with people further along their professional path; any of them could be a career ally at some point.

YOU MAY HAVE A DAY JOB YOU HATE.

Instead of focusing on the hatred, try to find something to like about the job. And if all else fails, focus on what it gives you, which is the means and the time to pursue what you ultimately want to do until you can make a living at it. Note: If the hated job doesn't allow you to pursue what you ultimately want to do, it's time to move on.

YOU WILL HEAR "*NO*" A *LOT* IN ONE FORM OR ANOTHER.

If you are an actor or musician, you will sometimes hear it to your face. TV producer Deb Spera (*Criminal Minds, Army Wives, Suspect Behavior*) says you should rejoice in the "no"s you get, that each "no" gets you that much closer to a "yes." That's easy to say when you are on her side of success, right? But you should appreciate that no successful person has ever gotten where he or she is in the biz by avoiding "no." And understand that Spera still hears "no" regularly, even at her level. The "no"s don't stop when you start making a living at your dream job. There are just more "yes"es mixed in.

YOU WILL HAVE TO TAKE FEEDBACK FROM PEOPLE OF QUESTIONABLE TASTE, AND SOME OF THAT FEEDBACK WILL BE TOTAL BULLSHIT.

You heard me. Total bullshit. Here's the thing you probably already know: Everyone thinks he or she is an expert when it comes to entertainment. And for performers and others who create, there is no end to the amount of feedback you hear. Even established and very successful entertainment pros (maybe even Beyoncé herself) have friends and extended family who call them up regularly to suggest some way they could do whatever it is they do better.

For those who are just starting out, there will be a lot of people in your path who may or may not be in a position to help you advance your career (often you will not know whether they are) who will critique your work. Some of it will be solicited feedback, and some of it will be kind and constructive. Some of it will be just plain mean or stupid or wrong. Suck it up and move on. Only time will tell if they will really be helpful to you, so you don't want to burn any bridges. But you also don't want to take destructive criticism to heart. Use what you can and dismiss the rest. Just like Beyoncé does when Great Aunt Esmeralda tells her that her dress was too short.

YOU WILL HAVE TO DEAL WITH YOUR LOVED ONES GROWING IMPATIENT.

Family members and friends who aren't in the business will have the impression that the leap from declaring your goal and achieving it is relatively short. Whether you are six months out of college or eight years out, these people will want to know when they'll see you (or your "written by" or "directed by" credit) on screen, when they'll hear you on the radio, when they can visit your windowed office on the studio lot. You may or may not want to engage in a detailed conversation about your progress. If you don't, just smile and say, "Soon... soon," and go get another serving of Thanksgiving turkey.

YOU WILL WONDER IF YOU WILL EVER MAKE IT.

You can really stress yourself out with this one. There will be a lot of uncertainty in the time between when you set a goal and when you reach it. Try to enjoy the process – and your life – while you do the work that will get you where you want to go professionally.

YOU MAY NOT MEET YOUR ORIGINAL GOAL.

It's true. Watch someone get voted out of one of those talent contest TV shows and you will see. Not everyone can win the prize. Here's the truth behind that one: In "not making it," there is no abyss. There is not death. There may be some version of your original dream and/or there is something else. You will not know what shape your life will take ten years down the line, what failures will end up being blessings, what seeming failures will turn into successes. But know that there is good stuff to be had in the future, whether it looks like your original vision or not.

Now that we've dispelled the myth of overnight success, let's turn our attention to the question of dream jobs and compatible day jobs.

CHAPTER 6
DREAM JOBS AND COMPATIBLE DAY JOBS

The day a senior executive came into my office to complain that his new assistant wanted time off in the middle of the day for an audition was a big eye-opener for me. The executive was thinking about the bidding war he was in for a hot script, with three other companies vying for it too. He was thinking about the big-budget movie he was overseeing whose star wouldn't come out of her trailer. He was thinking about the thirty-two phone calls he'd already gotten that morning that he needed to return. The last thing he needed was his new assistant demanding time off for an audition.

It was never in a million years going to happen, but he didn't need her distracted and mad the rest of the day because he had said no to her three-hour round-trip trek to the Valley for her possible big break. "Devon's an actress?" I asked, dumbfounded and a little annoyed. See, in my initial interview with Devon, I had asked her if she was an actress – as I'd asked almost every candidate since I'd started overseeing hiring for the company. Devon had assured me she was not an actress. Clearly she'd lied.

Hiring is a lot like matchmaking. If the boss you are screening candidates for likes long walks on the beach and reading Proust and you give him candidates who are avid sports fans and wouldn't know what "a Proust" was… well, you get the idea. The hiring version of this is that some positions need a real go-getter who is willing to work around the clock if necessary and wants to ultimately move up the executive ranks. Some positions require someone who can handle downtime and won't lose their minds if they aren't constantly busy. Some jobs have flexible hours. Some jobs do not. Jobs do not change to fit candidates and, as longtime hiring pros know, candidates do not change to fit jobs. The only good match is a good match.

It was a clear-cut situation for the executive and me. There was no way the terms of the job were going to change. Devon would either give up her auditioning or have to quit the job. In her case, as it turned out, it was a one-time problem. A friend had gotten her the opportunity to read for a project at his company. Though she would've liked to have gone, she wasn't going to jeopardize her job for it. So she stayed until she got a manager who was able to get her auditions regularly. At that point, she gave notice to the company and left on good terms. No surprises.

From that incident on, whenever I asked candidates about their dream pursuits, I explained why. "If you are actively auditioning, you don't want this job. You won't be able to leave during the work day for that," I would say, sometimes staring into their eyes to make my point clear. "Never. Ever." Or, "I find an aspiring writer works well in this position because they typically welcome a desk job that isn't too busy so they can work on their own projects." The aspiring writer's eyes would light up and I'd know that they were right for the position.

So what day jobs are compatible with which dream pursuits? Here's my rundown:

ASPIRING ACTOR/MUSICIAN/COMEDIAN

Restaurant/Nightclub Work/Hotel Work
There is a reason most waiters and bartenders are actors in Los Angeles. They need flexibility, which usually means having their days free when auditions come up and for filming, should they book the job. Waiting and bartending jobs, working for catering companies (catering is the temp version of waiting and bartending jobs), and working at hotels are usually compatible with the lives of aspiring actors. Key attributes: Flexible shifts, peer social interaction, the opportunity to meet industry insiders.

Downsides: Difficult to break into top places in Los Angeles and other cosmopolitan areas unless you look like a young Angelina Jolie/Brad Pitt. Often work vampire hours, especially at nightclubs. Hard on the feet. Also, if you are interested in doing theater at night, you would need to find a place that wouldn't require you to work then. (For this reason, the day shift would work for musicians who have gigs and standup comedians appearing in clubs – otherwise, it's not a fit.)

Administrative Temping
Temping is a great way to go when the market is strong and temps are in demand. If you have a special skill, such as accounting, or special training, such as paralegal certification, you might actually make a decent living.

Downsides: It might be hit and miss, at least until you prove yourself. (You want to be willing to go outside the entertainment industry to maximize your chances of consistent work when you are starting out.) Can be sporadic even for seasoned temps. Pay is sometimes low, especially for receptionist, data entry, Production Assistant, and any other low-skilled administrative work. Also, if you are actively auditioning, you will only be able to take last-minute temp gigs (covering when an employee calls in sick for that day, for instance) because you often find out about auditions only the day before they are held.

Virtual Assistant Work

Virtual assisting is a new trend, and with a lot of independent contractors and solo entrepreneurs out there who work from home and need administrative support but don't have a workspace for it, this is growing in popularity. Establishing yourself as a virtual assistant takes a little effort as you start out. You need to create a website and implement a social media strategy to promote your services in order to get and keep the work flowing in. But if you can get a few regular clients who have fairly large ongoing jobs and are willing to pay a decent hourly rate, this can be a good option.

Downsides: Requires some setup and initiative. If you just want to show up somewhere and get paid, this isn't for you. Also, it's a work-from-home situation, so if being in your apartment alone for more than a couple hours at a time drives you crazy, this is definitely a bad choice.

Bookkeeping, Social Media Marketer, Tech Troubleshooting, Dog Walking, etc.

These jobs are the in-person version of virtual assisting. You would be going to clients' homes to provide the services. As with virtual assisting, you need a way to market yourself and grow your business.

Downsides: If you live in a sprawling metropolis and hate to drive, look elsewhere for a good day job. Also requires setup and initiative. You will often spend as much time pursuing work opportunities as doing the work.

High-end Retail Selling

This can be lucrative, especially if you like talking to people and aren't put off by doing sales. Depending upon where you work, you can make a decent living and get the opportunity to meet potential industry contacts (while you sell them designer furniture or handbags).

Downsides: Of course, if you are not comfortable selling to people, this wouldn't be something to pursue. Also, landing the right opportunity in a weak economy can be challenging.

Fitness Trainer, Nutritionist, Masseuse, Yoga Instructor, Pilates Instructor, etc.

The health and wellness field attracts a lot of performers, and these are just some of the many positions that are popular. These positions can be regular jobs at fitness centers, spas, or holistic health centers, or they can be freelance work. People who prioritize staying fit and healthy often find this a compatible pursuit.

Downsides: All of these jobs require training and formal certification. And landing a well-paying "regular job version" of these positions can be challenging – though if you live in Los Angeles and network well, there are plenty of possibilities for employment and freelance work.

Childcare (Nanny, Babysitter)

This can be a good fit for those who are good with kids, as there are many working parents who need part-time or flexible childcare. A good nanny can work for a family for years, which can provide some measure of stability.

Downsides: Not the greatest pay, unless you are working for a very affluent family; often requires travel or night work.

ASPIRING WRITER/DIRECTOR/PRODUCER

Script Reading

Aspiring writers often turn to script reading to pay the bills while they create their own scripts and pursue writing opportunities. Studios and production companies employ freelance script readers to write coverage of material being submitted to the company. Experienced readers with good reputations are in demand. This is flexible in terms of being able to work from home, but often requires working on tight turnaround when the material under consideration is a hot property sought after by other companies, too.

Downsides: Breaking into script reading, especially for people who are new to the business and have a limited network, is very challenging. It can also be difficult for writers who are working on their own projects to keep a clear head when reading multiple other scripts per week. Lastly, if you are not a fast reader or writer, the hourly rate for this work can be abysmal.

Development Assistant Jobs

Aspiring writers/directors/producers often turn to working inside studios and production companies in the development departments for the education it affords them about how the industry works. They pursue their own projects on the side, when time allows. For aspiring producers, though, moving up in the development and production departments inside a company can be a fantastic way to develop producing skills at the highest level and make the type of contacts a producer needs to get projects made.

Downsides: Development assistant positions are hard to come by, and you typically need an "in" at a company, since those openings almost never make it to the open market. Also, these jobs usually involve long hours and taking scripts home to read off-hours. It can be a challenge to find time for side projects, especially once you move out of the administrative role and into the junior executive ranks.

General/Other Administrative Jobs

As mentioned at the beginning of this chapter, administrative positions that involve a lot of downtime, such as receptionist or assistant on a sporadically busy desk, afford aspiring writers the opportunity to work on their own scripts while at work. Even administrative positions that don't provide the downtime for assistants to work on their own material can be good for aspiring writers, directors, and producers as long as the hours are limited and they are able to have plenty of non-work time to write and/or shoot their own projects. The consistency of a steady paycheck and having benefits such as health insurance and sick leave can be very good for a creative who is able to pursue his or her dream outside typical office hours.

Downsides: This one is pretty downside-free, as long as the parameters of the job are clear and the hours truly are limited. Even administrative positions outside the industry are good day jobs, though it's nice for creative people to be in creative environments. Take that into consideration when seeking administrative work.

Production Assistant Jobs/Other Crew Work

Working in production can be a good option for the aspiring writer, director, or producer, too. The idea is that you work fourteen-hour days making good money for a couple of days or months, depending upon whether you are working on commercials or TV shows/films, and then have time off between gigs to focus on your own work. The bonus for aspiring directors is that you are meeting crewmembers who may be willing to work on your own projects. (The second camera assistant on a big studio movie might welcome the opportunity to be your cinematographer, for example.)

Downsides: The feast-or-famine nature of freelance crew work might not fit with everyone's temperament. When you are working, you are working all the time, and when you are not, you might be preoccupied with where your next gig is coming from. The ability to compartmentalize and truly devote time and energy to your own pursuits when you are not working is the key to making this day job situation workable for you.

Crossover Jobs from the Aspiring Actor/Musician/Comedian Section

There are a few options from the list for aspiring actors and other performers that can also work for aspiring writers, directors, and producers. Of course, waiting and bartending can work for anyone as a day job, though the same difficulties breaking into the top places apply and also the same issues for non–night owls and people who want their nights free for other things.

Virtual assisting, health and wellness positions, high-end retail, or having some kind of "solopreneur" business, such as bookkeeping, can also work for the aspiring writer, as long as a steady workflow is maintained. As with any day job, you don't want your energy focused on making a living while you are trying to pursue your dreams. That is why I think that unless you need some of your days free for classes or for some other reason, temping as a permanent job is a mistake for writers, directors, and producers. The flexibility actors need requires that they consider temping as an option, but if you don't need the flexibility, finding a stable position will serve you better.

CHAPTER 7
STABILITY AND PARALLEL CAREERS

In an interview with *Criminal Minds* creator Jeff Davis on TheScriptLab.com, the interviewer noted that Davis famously had no backup plan should his writing aspirations have failed to pan out. She then pointed out that if everyone's pitches and spec pilots were bought, there wouldn't be enough television stations to air them, and she asked Davis what kinds of backup plans people should have in place. He replied, "What I usually say to would-be writers is that if you want a career in Hollywood, don't have a backup plan. Persistence is actually just as important as talent, and if you want to succeed in this business, you have to give yourself over to it completely."

"So, when should one give up?" the interviewer asks. Davis replies, "Never. Not if you truly want a career in this business. The only time I would ever give up is if everyone around you told you bluntly and repeatedly that you are the worst writer to have ever walked the face of the Earth. And even then I wouldn't give up. Van Gogh never sold a painting in his life."

Things worked well for Davis, making it easy for him to give the "have no backup plan" advice. But I think we can all agree that Vincent van Gogh is not a good role model for many reasons, the most relevant of which is that he died at age 38 (by a self-inflicted gunshot wound to the chest, but that's another story). These days, people live about twice that long or longer. Thirty more years struggling to get your first paycheck in your dream pursuit would be quite a long haul. And even if it didn't take that long, some people don't want to put off being able to build a "real" life for themselves, sometimes with spouses and kids who require things like health insurance and diapers, which do not come cheap.

So when does a day job become a parallel career? Beyond day jobs are what some people call "real jobs" and I call "career jobs." I differentiate day jobs from career jobs in that a career job allows for professional growth, so even some of the jobs in the previous chapters would qualify as parallel careers depending upon how they were pursued. For instance, a bookkeeper could develop an ongoing clientele that would provide "real life" money and potentially lead to hiring associates to help with the workload and grow the revenue. But if you are a bookkeeper who lets that business drop when you have acting income or another money-making opportunity, that is a day job.

Actress Carey Peters became a Certified Holistic Health Coach through the Institute for Integrative Medicine in addition to auditioning and studying acting. She developed a nutritional consulting business and then added coaching other nutritional coaches on how to build their businesses to her professional roster. These days, she appears with Judy Greer in the "Reluctantly Healthy" video series on Yahoo TV in addition to running her "Lose Weight Like a Celebrity" weight loss program and her "Holistic MBA" coaching program. Oh, and she still takes acting jobs when she is available.

One of the secrets of being a working entertainment professional is that the vast majority do not actually "make it" and then never have to worry about money again. Most people, even actors who are in series and writers whose screenplays have been optioned by studios and sometimes even made into films, have flush years and lean years.

Writer Sterling Anderson, who was profiled on YourIndustryInsider.com in December 2011, hit a brick wall in his successful career writing TV movies of the week. Around the time of the 9/11 attacks, when he had just bought a nice home in an upscale Los Angeles neighborhood, his six-figure income disappeared almost overnight. Tightened network budgets coupled with the popularity of the relatively cheap new reality genre led to the rapid demise of the TV movie.

Lucky for Anderson, the woman who had just sold him his house and become a friend in the process happened to own an animation production company – and she welcomed him as creator and writer of new shows for the company. From there, he transitioned into writing for one-hour TV dramas, which remains his primary genre today. He has also done some teaching and speaking, so had he not gotten into animation, he had other ways to go. But for many, a shift in the industry can be devastating.

Whether it's something extreme, like what happened in Anderson's case or in the case of a prolonged labor strike, or a just a normal lull in work opportunities, lean times can be highly stressful. Some people are forced to return to bartending or administrative work. Others have to come up with a new line of work in their thirties, forties, or beyond.

A compatible "career job" developed as someone is beginning to pursue his or her dreams in entertainment can provide both a backup if things don't work out and an alternative should the work dry up or become unsatisfying midcareer. In the ideal world, not only does the parallel career provide more stability, it also involves some kind of passion.

Actor/comedian Ken Jeong (*The Hangover* movies, *Community*) studied and then practiced medicine first in New Orleans and then in Los Angeles. He performed standup on the side, until he broke through as an actor. He has said he enjoyed being a doctor and still keeps his license current in case he should need to go back to it.

In some cases, the stable career job and the dream pursuit can somehow merge. In actress Carey Peters' case, a health issue led to an interest in wellness that led to getting formal training. And eventually her nutritional work merged with acting – hence, the Yahoo series and other web and television opportunities to discuss her nutritional work, which utilizes her on-camera chops.

Also worth noting is that in some cases, the parallel career path actually facilitates the aspirant's entry into entertainment. For instance, David E. Kelley was a practicing attorney who wrote on the side when he landed his first staff writing job. That first gig was on *L.A. Law*, and he was hired because Steven Bochco was looking for writers with legal backgrounds. Kelley has undoubtedly gotten more than enough out of his study of law by developing several legal-themed one-hour dramas such as *Ally McBeal, The Practice, Boston Legal, and Harry's Law*.

Your day job can turn into a parallel career path and inspire your creative work, as was the case with Nick Offerman from TV's *Parks & Recreation*. A skilled woodworker, he had made money building scenery in Chicago early in his career. Soon after moving to Los Angeles, he opened Offerman Woodshop (www.offermanwoodshop.com), which makes small boats and furniture and employs several people besides Nick.

When the writers on *Parks & Recreation* found out about Nick's passion for woodcraft, his character became a skilled woodworker as well. It is one of the defining characteristics of Ron Swanson *and* a source of income he still has today. Think about the opportunity to have that kind of synergy (or Carey Peters' or David E. Kelley's) at work in your career!

ACTION PROMPT 5

Determine your needs and identify options for day jobs
and parallel careers.

This Action Prompt applies to those of you who need to support yourself
while you pursue something creative, like acting, directing, or writing,
even if you already have a day job you think is working for you. (Is it
really working for you? Could it be a parallel career? Let's find out.)

Day Job
To figure out a day job, you must be clear about what you need to support
yourself and pursue your dream. Answer these questions:

1) How much money do you need to make per month to cover your living
   expenses? (If you don't know how much your monthly living expenses
   are, it's time to do some research.)

2) What time(s) do you need available to pursue your creative dreams?
   If you are a writer, unless you write with a partner and need to sync
   schedules with him or her, or unless you work with a theater group or
   otherwise need to be at a certain place at a certain time for your
   writing, you are probably open.

   If you are an actor, your need for availability will depend on whether
   you are getting auditions, in which case you need to be free during the
   day, and/or doing theater or taking classes, which generally means you
   must be free in the evening.

   If you need to be available during the day, you need to look at the
   night work. If you need to be available in the evenings, you need to look
   at day work options. If you need flexibility both times, you need to find
   work that can be done around your schedule.

3) What do you like to do? Go back to the brain dump from Action Prompt
   1 and see if you can find any clues from that.

4) Review Chapter 6, "Dream Jobs and Compatible Day Jobs" and jot down any options that may work.

5) If the promising options involve training that you don't have right now, such as for bookkeeping or paralegal work, research training programs and consider if they are feasible.

Parallel Career

So how do you come up with a parallel career path? Well, you know when a big movie star is being interviewed and he or she is asked, "What would you have done if you weren't a big movie star?" Pretend that's you. Or look at the list of potential day jobs you just created (or consider your current day job) and ask, "What's the six-figure version of this?" That should get you started.

Again, you'll want to research any training you would need to get in order to follow this parallel career path and create a timeline (you may need to have a plain old day job while you get this career path going).

If creating a parallel career path sounds like a lot of extra work for someone who is passionate about a creative pursuit, think about how nice it would be to have something else to firmly support you so you can rest easily and choose what projects to work on without stressing about being able to pay your bills every month. Plus, you never know how it's going to pay off in the long run, such as enabling or enhancing your creative pursuits.

ENTERTAINMENT CAREER PLANNING CHECKLIST

Review of Phase One

ACTION PROMPT 1

____ You made a big uncensored list of things you love. Add to it whenever you want.

ACTION PROMPT 2

____ You defined your "what."

____ You examined your "why."

____ You identified your practical considerations.

ACTION PROMPT 3

(Skip if you already know your "where.")

____ You determined which places you might want to live.

____ You made a list of factors affecting your decision.

____ You used the Weighted Average Decision Matrix (WADM) or some other method to determine the winner.

ACTION PROMPT 4

____ You looked on the Internet, read books, and watched TV shows and documentaries about your desired job or field.

____ You spoke with people directly about your desired job or field.

____ You found a way to test-drive your ambition (and, with any luck, are doing it!).

ACTION PROMPT 5

(Skip if your goal involves a "career job" and you do not need an alternative source of income or if you already have a parallel career. Otherwise, these exercises are mandatory.)

____ You went through the day job questions.

____ You reviewed Chapter 6 and made note of any that might work.

____ You brainstormed parallel career paths, whether they are some "exploded" version of the day job options or an alternative professional path.

PHASE TWO: READYING YOUR RESOURCES

They say you go to war with the army you have, not the army you wish you had. Usually they say this when trying to explain away defeat. In other words, "It wasn't my fault. Look at these guys!" In this war, your army is the arsenal of resources and tools that you strategically deploy to help you reach your objectives and conquer your goal list.

For this first battle of the war – breaking in – you need to identify what resources you have at your disposal and how to acquire more, as well as learning how best to use them. You also need to prepare the tools (I will refrain from calling them weapons) you will use to find and land job opportunities and build a career with maximum potential for growth and satisfaction. These tools are your job hunt materials, your web presence, and your pitch.

By the end of this section, you will have lined up resources and tools you can be proud of. And by using them, you can celebrate victories and, despite the inevitable setbacks and course corrections that come into every-one's careers, never have to face true defeat.

CHAPTER 8
WHO ARE YOU, AND WHAT DO YOU HAVE TO OFFER?

Years ago, I was involved in a mentoring organization. My mentee was a smart young woman named Maria who was prone to making dramatic proclamations while we were driving around Los Angeles in my car. "I don't know what I want to do with my life!" she lamented during one of those car rides the summer between her freshman and sophomore years of college. I told her that she didn't need to know, that most people don't know when they are at her phase of life. That seemed to calm her down, as was my usual practice during these moments.

Sure enough, eventually she chose a major and graduated from college. The following summer, during another one of our car rides, we talked about her job search. "Do you know what type of organization you'd like to work for?" I asked. She spoke about her different options, about what the school counselor had suggested, about what her family thought. "I just know I don't want to do any administration," she said with a tone of finality. "What do you mean?" I asked. "You know. Filing… copying…" She trailed off. "Maria," I told her gently, "you're not qualified to do anything else."

Now some of you might feel that what I told this new grad was harsh, or that I was undermining her confidence by telling her that filing and making copies were all anyone should pay her to do, dooming her to a lifetime of low work-place self-esteem and menial labor. She went to a good school, studied hard, and earned her degree, right?

A brand-new graduate with a newly minted diploma is a wondrous thing. College expands a young mind and often puts lofty goals in there. But, as I explained to Maria, while it's important to aim high, if you are just out of college, you must be willing to do a little grunt work at first. The semi-crappy first job is an earn-while-you-learn opportunity, a chance to figure out how your industry works and how the organization you work for works, and to develop whatever skills or qualities will get you away from the copier.

I went to a good college, too, and studied hard, though (full disclosure) probably not as hard as Maria did. I earned a degree in Broadcasting and Film and landed the all-important foot-in-the-door job. But when I showed up for my first day on the movie set, nobody escorted me over to the camera and asked me what I thought the shot should look like or handed me a copy of the budget to see where I thought it could be tightened. They put a walkie-talkie in my hand and told me to stand outside the door to the bar they were shooting in and make sure nobody tried to enter it.

While I was standing there on my first day in showbiz, I watched the grips walk by with their C-stands and heard the walkie-talkie chatter of the gaffers executing the lighting directives of the cinematographer. I learned what Craft Services was and that the drivers are usually happy to chat with a new Production Assistant, but the producers are not.

So how did I take that first step up from the entry level? As luck would have it, the Second Second Assistant Director (yes, that's a title – look it up) noticed that I guarded the door to the bar without question or complaint, even though everyone knew it was locked from the inside. (I actually had questioned the assignment – to someone else – and was told someone knocking on the door or even rattling the handle could ruin the take if they were filming inside when it happened. Fair enough.)

Anyway, they had one general PA too many, so he asked me what areas of the film set I was interested in finding out more about. I told him the Prop Department looked interesting. So he walked me over to where the Prop Master and her assistant were going through a tray of sunglasses for the lead actor, selecting a few pairs for the director to choose from. "Do you guys need any help?" the Second Second asked them. "Sure," the Prop Master said. And thus I got my first promotion, just days into my entertainment career.

Which brings me to the six core things of value that facilitate your career progression. I call these things "Hollywood currency," and they exist everywhere in entertainment, and most of them apply to other fields, too. The six kinds of Hollywood currency are: knowledge, relationships, expertise, quid pro quo, cash, and talent. Here's how they are all defined in this context:

Knowledge = "Who's who and what's what?"

How many major studios are there, and what are they? Who's Adam McKay? How do you get a PA job on a movie? What does a talent agent do? Study up and ask a lot of questions when you are starting out, and you can accrue some of this currency pretty quickly. (And lucky you, there's a lot of knowledge to be gained by just reading this book!)

Relationships = "Who do you know, and who do they know?"

It's the key to landing a job in any field these days, but it's especially important in a competitive field where the plum jobs don't often get posted online. It's also vital to pursuing your dream jobs. As an actress, relationships can be used to get an audition for a part you'd be perfect for or a meeting with an agent. As a writer, you won't get in the room to pitch a project to a potential buyer if you don't have an "in." For directors, costume designers, editors, production company executives, and on down the line to that entry-level Production Assistant job, it's who you know that often gets you work and creative opportunity.

Expertise = "What do you know how to do?"

One dictionary definition is "having, involving, or displaying special skill or knowledge derived from training or experience." You will probably arrive in Hollywood with some expertise – for instance, how to reconcile a checking account on Quicken, how to coach kids to be excellent junior tennis players, how to produce a student film. Being able to create a feature movie budget, light a scene on a soundstage, sell the overseas distribution rights to an independent movie – these are examples of Hollywood expertise that you can bank on. As you climb the ladder and prove yourself, you will be able to first observe and then execute these types of tasks as you develop your skill at them. If you show initiative and focus on doing a great job at whatever you are given, opportunities will come to you more quickly.

Which brings me to this equation: Knowledge + Relationships + Expertise = a job offer.

By the end of my first Production Assistant job, I had knowledge of how a film set worked ("Who's who and what's what?"), relationships with many crewmembers, including the Property Master and her assistant, and some expertise about props. And, as you'll recall if you read my story at the beginning of the book, I would be called a few months later to be the Assistant Prop Master on a movie that Prop Master was doing in L.A.

Okay, let's cover the other three forms of Hollywood currency:

Quid Pro Quo = "Who owes you what?"

Quid pro quo is defined as "something for something; that which a party receives (or is promised) in return for something he does or gives or promises." Hollywood runs on quid pro quo. Having someone owe you a favor is like having money in the bank. It's also a great way to cement yourself in someone's mind. (Note: In some contexts, quid pro quo refers to someone asking for sex in exchange for something, such as a job promotion or a chance at a part in a movie. You'll want to pass on that type of quid pro quo. Find another way.)

Cash = "How much you got?"

If you can come to town a dot-com or real estate billionaire or the offspring of a dry cleaning magnate, to some extent, you just have to introduce yourself and your big pile of money to a few people and the industry will come to you. But though you can buy your way into the entertainment world with cold, hard moolah by bankrolling an indie movie, producing a record, or investing in a start-up entertainment company, eventually you'll have to start trading in other forms of currency to have a real career.

Talent = "How can you move me?"

Talent is defined as "a marked innate ability, as for artistic accomplishment." And yes, some people are born with (or demonstrate early on) certain qualities, such as the ability to carry a tune or a natural five-octave range that, if developed, could result in a great singer. A great sense of story or an eye for composition could result in a great writer or cinematographer. But undeveloped, these qualities are just potential, and even with developed talent and none of the other forms or currency, it's going to be hard to gain a foothold in the industry.

Think about it. You can write a fantastic script or direct a groundbreaking no-budget short film, but without getting it read or seen, respectively, by the right people, your talent isn't going to get you out of living in your parents' basement, much less onto the awards podium. You need other forms of Hollywood currency to realize your creative dreams and even your business dreams. You don't need all forms of currency, but you will need at least one to get you started on your path.

A good example of someone putting it all together and growing a career is C.P. Roth, who was profiled on YourIndustryInsider.com in late 2011. He's an accomplished rock musician with a long career that has included session work and touring with some of the top acts over the years, as well as being a founding member of Blessid Union of Souls. He's currently a member of the Liza Colby Sound, as well as a member and musical director for comedian Denis Leary's touring band, The Enablers. He's a frequent guest musician at gigs for popular bands around New York and elsewhere.

But when he was just out of music school and living in New York, even though he'd been playing gigs since he was a teenager and had had a couple of small jobs in the music business, he didn't have much currency. He needed a day job, as well as a way into the New York professional music scene. As luck would have it, the music store he'd been hanging out in while he was a student, Manny's Music, a central hub of the music business, needed a drum tech, which is basically someone who could recommend and sell drums.

C.P. was a drummer (knowledge, expertise) and was already friendly with the owner and the other guys who worked at the store (relationships), so he got the job. On top of that, starting as a teen, C.P. had studied analogue synthesizer technology, which was brand-new at the time, so he became Manny's first synthesizer salesperson. Working at Manny's, playing around, and getting some session work under his belt (more relationships, more knowledge, and I'm sure he did favors for lots of people – he's a nice guy – so quid pro quo, too), he established his name as a top synthesizer player, one of the few at the time. (Bonus points to C.P. for having rare and highly sought-after expertise. As you can read in his profile, that expertise led to some serious career progress, not to mention getting to meet and spend a few hours with his hero, John Lennon.)

ACTION PROMPT 6

Identify "Who are you, and what do you have to offer?"

Setting aside relationships and quid pro quo (we're going to cover them in detail in the next chapter), I want you to break down the other four categories of currency and identify what you have now in terms of each one, as it applies to whatever job and/or passion you are pursuing right now. Also, identify areas where getting more of one type of currency as soon as possible will help you move forward quicker.

Knowledge = "Who's who and what's what?"

Start with what you know about the industry's products. Do you know about every reality TV show that ever aired? Romantic comedy? Book adaptations? Video games? Now what about knowledge of the industry? Have you worked on a film before? Do you already know who does what? Did you intern at a TV network? Did you submit your short film to every LGBT-related film festival in the country? Knowing what those festivals are counts as part of your knowledge base.

Some can be used on your résumé, in a cover letter, or in a job interview. (Encyclopedic reality TV knowledge is definitely worth noting in your cover letter and bringing up in an interview when applying to a reality TV production company.) Some of your knowledge can help you come up with strategies for your career, and what opportunities to pursue, and some of it can help other people with their goals, which makes you more valuable in the entertainment community.

Expertise = "What do you know how to do?"

What do you know how to do? In the example in the "Knowledge" section above, the person who knows about all the LGBT-related film festivals because he or she submitted a film to them actually has expertise in submitting films to LGBT-related festivals. You may be surprised at what kind of knowledge you have accumulated by the time you graduated from college or are a couple of years out. Have you budgeted and shot short films? Did you create a social media campaign for your college fundraising drive? Can you do website design? This all counts. Write it down – and anything else that might come in handy in a job hunt, a day job hunt, or in building your reputation and value in the industry.

Cash = "How much have you got?"

Yes, count your money, but if you do have money to potentially spend on a creative project, I would recommend cultivating relationships and getting the lay of the land in the industry before you use it. It will get you further if you are very strategic and deliberate about where it goes and if you have a little know-how before you open up the coffers.

Talent = "How can you move me?"

Can you sing? Dance? Do improvisation? Tell jokes? Create great stories? Great, but don't get too excited. Without the five other types of currency, it can be challenging to get anywhere with talent, no matter how much of it you have. Yes, write them down and keep working on them, but definitely don't isolate yourself from the industry until you feel that they are perfectly honed and you are ready to share them. Gather knowledge and develop your expertise in a lot of areas. Look for opportunities to build a community and a network. Talent doesn't just emerge fully formed from a closet to be greeted by millions of cheering fans. It takes time.

Don't be discouraged if you feel you don't have much to include in this exercise. In a few years, when you look back from down the road, you will see the accumulation of this currency in your own career story. Let's delve deeper into two of the most valuable and easily gained forms.

CHAPTER 9
IDENTIFYING AND BUILDING YOUR NETWORK

At the beginning of her career, Debbie Liebling was a producer at the then fledgling New York–based cable channel MTV. An office down the hall was occupied by a young actor named Ben Stiller who had a show on the channel. He and Debbie used to hang out and chat during downtime. Debbie went on to head programming for Comedy Central and occupy several high-level studio film production executive positions. Ben Stiller has starred in many big movies, of course, such as *There's Something About Mary, Meet the Parents, Tropic Thunder,* and *Night at the Museum.* Also a director and producer, a little over a decade ago, he co-founded a film production company called Red Hour, which is based at Sony Pictures.

A couple of years ago, he brought Debbie in to head up a new TV division at the company. Though she had worked on a few movies starring and produced by Stiller over the course of her years as a studio production executive, she partially credits that time twenty-five years ago in the hallways of MTV with giving him the trust level to hire her for the position she has now. This story illustrates that the entertainment industry is made up of a web of relationships and the longer you are in it, the larger and more densely woven your network is.

I experienced firsthand the positive and negative effect of this interconnected-ness. I have mentioned a couple of times in this book, including in the previous chapter, that during my first Production Assistant job on a movie, I had the op-portunity to work in the Prop Department. The Prop Master ended up hiring me for another movie a few months later. That's an example where forming a good relationship paid off. I found out later, though, that the Prop Master almost had to take back the job offer for the second movie because a producer on the first movie was the producer of the second movie and she told my would-be boss she didn't think I could do the job.

The truth was that I had been rude to that producer because I thought she had been rude to me. Ultimately, she allowed the Prop Master to hire me, and I made an effort to be extra-polite and helpful to the producer from then on.

She never became particularly warm to me, but I learned from how she treated other people that she was not deliberately snubbing me. She was busy and preoccupied with her producing responsibilities.

WHO DO YOU KNOW?

Sometimes that's a hard question to answer. When you're in your early twenties and/or trying to launch a career in a new field, it's especially difficult. "I don't know anyone!" you scream inside, thinking that your entertainment industry contacts have to be IN the entertainment industry. Don't get stuck on that stipulation. This question is really a two-parter whose second part is often left unsaid: "Who do you know – and who do they know?"

For instance, if you know me and you ask me for help, but I can't supply what you need (a job, an "in" at a company, etc.), I might reach out to my contacts. Those contacts through me are your second-degree connections. It's like the old game "Six Degrees of Kevin Bacon," where every other actor was connected to actor Kevin Bacon by the movies they had been in together. (Examples: Tommy Lee Jones is a first-degree connection to Kevin Bacon because they were in *JFK* together. George Clooney is a second-degree connection because he was in *Oceans 11* with Julia Roberts, who was in *Flatliners* with Kevin Bacon, but he has not been in a movie with Kevin Bacon.)

In Hollywood, everyone is playing the relationship game. When you are starting out, most likely you only have second-degree connections. You probably don't know film producer Brian Grazer personally, unless you went to school with one of his kids, but the guy who runs your college summer internship program might know someone who can get you an interview for a Production Assistant job at Brian Grazer's company, Imagine Entertainment.

When TV writer Eric Rogers (*Futurama, Brickleberry*), who was profiled on YourIndustryInsider.com in 2012, was in high school, he met his mother's boss's daughter at an event and found out she was a TV writer/producer (Ann Donahue, *Picket Fences, Murder One*, and the *CSI franchise*). When he expressed interest in being a TV writer, she told him to get his college degree and then get in touch with her during his senior year of college if he still wanted to write for TV. That one fateful meeting led to him getting his first job in television, as a Production Assistant on a new show coming out from then-top TV producer Steven Bochco. One meeting with one person who came through someone completely unaffiliated with the entertainment industry launched Eric's career.

CREATING YOUR ENTERTAINMENT NETWORK LIST

Here are some examples of people you already know: Your classmates, your professors, people you interned with and for, your parents' friends, your older siblings' friends, the girl who used to babysit for you whose boyfriend at the time left to go work on a movie in L.A. You also know your college's career counselor and someone a couple of years ahead of you in school who was the composer on an indie film that premiered at Sundance. And so on.

When you look at your network list, you might wonder if these people will re-member you. Some of them you know, some you only *met* a couple of times. Don't cross anyone out, though. When you reach out, you can always start with, "I don't know if you remember me but…" You may be surprised at how many people reply, "Of *course* I remember you" and follow up with a quick, "So, what can I do for you?" If they don't remember you or if they brush you off or don't reply, try not to take it personally. Not everyone will help. And you only need one or two key "ins" to get your start. Be polite if met with rejection, and move on to the next person in your list.

DO YOURSELF A FAVOR AND DO SOMEONE A FAVOR

Now that we have a strategy for getting you into the industry, let's make sure that moving forward, you build strong relationship foundations. How do you establish the kind of rapport with people you meet socially or work with even for a short time where they remember you and even become part of your network? Of course, it starts with being polite and open, and doing your job well when you are working. Showing interest in other people is also vital. You may think your story is fascinating, or that you only have a couple of minutes to find out if they can help you with whatever you need at the time, but you are better served to focus on them and what they are up to, and let the "ask" wait.

Some people call this networking – and it is, at its basic level. But your entertain-ment career will be a long and twisting road, and what you are really doing is making friends who will be along for the ride. Yes, you will likely need an "in" for most jobs and other opportunities you get and you may be focused on the one you need NOW, but most people you meet won't be helpful NOW; they will be helpful later. (Think of Debbie Liebling and the job she got twenty-five years after hanging out with the nice young actor in the halls of fledgling MTV.)

But how can you be sure they will remember you when you need them? First of all, follow up meeting them by reaching out online and with adding them to your LinkedIn connections. Also, touch base every so often to see what they are up to and maybe arrange an in-person meeting. There's nothing like a coffee date to cement a relationship.

Beyond that is that other form of Hollywood currency I mentioned earlier, quid pro quo. It is most easily defined as trading favors. "I got that guy's script read by a Creative Executive at Walden Media. In return, he's going to hook me up with an interview in the Paramount marketing department." "That woman got my niece an internship at Will Smith's company. So now she's calling to see if I can get Justin Timberlake tickets for her daughter." It's not usually that immediate and often not that calculated (though sometimes it is), but over the course of your career, you will do many favors and have many favors done for you.

Now, you may ask, early in your career (or even before you have landed your first job), what could you possibly be in a position to do for someone else? If you're still in school, you could offer to help your film studies professor assemble reading materials for the class. (You might already do that. Let's hope you're just that kind of helpful person.) If you're out of school, you could volunteer at your college's alumni association events or your city's film festival. You might offer to crew for free on your internship coordinator's weekend short film shoot.

Here's an example of something anyone could definitely do: If you are "in your element," such as at a social gathering where you know most of the people, and you see someone new who doesn't know the group, take the opportunity to introduce yourself and find out who that person is. You will put him or her at ease and potentially make a friend for life just by shaking hands and initiating conversation. No money spent, no industry connections needed – just a nice, normal, human moment. And you never know who that ill-at-ease stranger might turn out to be, at the time or in the future.

So to build that network quickly, reach out to new people and stay in touch with those you already know. Make some friends in entertainment and then do yourself a favor and do them all a favor. See how quickly your relationship currency – and your quid pro quo currency – add up!

ACTION PROMPT 7

Make your entertainment networking list.

Open your computer file to get you started on your path to knowing everyone in the industry.

NOTE: This is the beginning of a multi-step process that will continue as you advance in your career, so I recommend starting an Excel workbook with this list as your first page, but if you prefer MS Word or another program, that will work as well.

Start with your hometown. Who from your childhood might know someone in the industry who could be helpful? Think about high school classmates, your parents' friends, and other adults. Now go through college: Your roommates over the years, people from the dorm, people you had classes with, especially those you worked on projects with, professors, internship coordinators and peers, bosses and co-workers at any jobs you had in school. Now go post-graduate, assuming you are out of school, and think of co-workers, of people you socialize with and the friends of your friends whom you have met but have not yet become full-fledged friends with.

Write down all those names, along with a note about who they are and how you know them. (You will be referring to – and adding to – this list for a long time and though they might be fresh in mind now, your memory of them might fade. The note will come in handy.) Include second-degree contacts even if you have never met them and even never have the chance of meeting them. They could come in handy regardless. Don't edit, even if you barely know some of these people. You won't necessarily reach out now, but something may come up that makes reaching out to them a good idea. If they aren't on the list, you might not remember to contact them.

Think About What You Can Do for Them

It seems calculated, and to some extent it is, but it's also about appreciating other people, especially people who are further along in their careers and therefore are asked for favors a lot. When someone takes the time to have an interview with you (either informational or for an actual job), the least you can do is send him or her a thank-you email and even a snail-mail thank-you note. And if someone recommends you for a freelance gig, at the very least, a thank you is called for there as well.

You won't always have something you can do for the people you know in your professional life, but give it some thought. Even if you do it every once in a while, you will get a reputation for being thoughtful and grateful and nice. And who doesn't want to help thoughtful, grateful, nice people?

	A	B	C	D
1	NAME	POSITION / TITLE	RELATIONSHIP	NOTE
2	Professor Laraby	Screenwriting professor	took 3 of her classes	She was a creative executive at a studio in LA a few years ago.
3	Liz Jones	Director of Development, Jim Henson Prods	internship coordinator	Told me to get in touch when I got back to Los Angeles
4	Martin Bradford	TV writer	mom's friend's son	Worked on "Glee," currently on a pilot
5	Marcy Brown	Production Asst - production company	college friend	Find out what company
6	Elliot Wigg	Temping	college friend	
7	Jeff Allen	Assistant at Blue Grass Entertainment	friend from HS	Not sure if he's still there - reconnect?
8				
9				
10				
11				
12				
13				
14				
15				
16				
17				
18				
19				
20				
21				
22				
23				
24				
25				
26				
27				
28				
29				
30				
31				

Networking List   Network Tracking Sheet   Job Hunt Resource List   Job Hunt Tracking Shee

CHAPTER 10
STELLAR ENTERTAINMENT RÉSUMÉS

A lot of people think the traditional résumé is going the way of low-definition TV. But rumors of its demise are mostly being spread by companies touting pricey alternatives, such as video résumés and web career apps. Whether it lives online or is a stand-alone PDF document emailed to recruiters or hiring executives as a targeted career summary and record of accomplishments, the résumé can't be beat and isn't going anywhere.

> There are certain positions in the entertainment industry that don't require a traditional fleshed-out résumé. Actors, directors, and production personnel who are responsible for some tangible aspect of the finished product (such as costumes, production design, editing, the score) have résumés that list basic information about projects they've worked on and include a link to a site with a reel and/or a portfolio of photos that highlight their best work.

Like many seasoned hiring professionals, I can tell more about you by reading your employment submission (email, cover letter, and résumé) than most people get from a thirty-minute interview. Everything from your email address to the length of the document to the professional summary you put at the top of your résumé (or not) tells me whether or not you're a promising contender for the job I have to fill – or *any* job, for that matter.

THE THREE PILES

I have reviewed thousands of résumés during my career. Some have gotten only a cursory glance and a trip to the literal or virtual trashcan (aka the "no" pile). Some have gotten a closer look and a spot in the "maybe" pile. Only a small number earn a coveted place in the "yes" pile, meaning, "Yes, your story interests me. Yes, I think you're a contender. Yes, I want to meet you face-to-face."

Here's what lands your résumé in the trashcan or "no" pile:

★ Sloppiness or a professional summary block clearly written for some other job. (Message: "I don't pay attention to my work.")

★ An out-of-town address. (Message: "I *might* be moving to Los Angeles.")

★ No qualifying experience listed and no professional summary block explaining how unrelated experience applies to this job. (Message: "I'm hoping I'm the only applicant.")

Here's what lands your résumé in the "maybe" pile:

★ An otherwise stellar résumé with the slightly wrong background, such as being overqualified in another, related field. (Message: "I am trying to make a career transition and don't mind taking a step back for the right opportunity.")

★ An otherwise stellar résumé from someone who is a little under-qualified, such as having a couple of great internships but no paid jobs for a non-entry-level position. (Message: "I am a confident go-getter hoping you'll recognize my potential.")

Here's what lands your résumé in the "yes" pile:

★ A stellar résumé with relevant experience listed or a stellar résumé with slightly unrelated experience and a professional summary block that explains how your background and skills relate to the demands of this position. (Message: "I am qualified, motivated, and attentive to detail. You can hire me and feel confident I will get the job done right.")

RULES FOR STELLAR RÉSUMÉS

Okay, so what is a "stellar résumé," anyway? Below, you will find some fundamentals and a breakdown of key elements. But first, here are the "Rules for Résumés" I developed during my fifteen-plus years as a hiring executive and five-plus years as a professional résumé writer:

Résumé Rule #1 – A Résumé Is a Marketing Tool, Not a Career History.

A résumé is NOT a comprehensive career history; it's an advertisement for a candidate for a specific job, whether that job is Production Assistant, Marketing Coordinator, Vice President of Finance, or Executive Assistant to a Talent Agent. Whenever possible, you should customize your résumé, highlighting the experience, skills, and expertise you have that most apply to the requirements of the job. In a highly competitive field, the more laser-focused your résumé, the better your chances are of getting an interview. In fact, often a laser-focused résumé is your only chance.

NOTE: Yes, that means you need more than one résumé if you are searching for more than one type of job. If you are seeking a Production Assistant job on a set OR an Administrative Assistant job at a talent agency, you should ideally have two documents, one of which highlights any on-set experience you have had (even while in school) and draws attention to transferrable skills from other jobs related to the requirements of the PA job (running errands, completing miscellaneous projects, etc.). The other résumé should highlight office experience and draw attention to skills related to those job requirements (phone work, customer service, etc). You will likely include all of your work experience in both documents, but switch up the emphasis depending upon the position.

Résumé Rule #2 – A Résumé Should Have a Compelling Narrative.
Yes, there is a story on your résumé. For instance: "Ivy League graduate who went to law school and then worked at a talent agency before moving into physical production." "Recent grad with two impressive internships and a long-term part-time server job during school interested in pursuing a career in television" is another story. Both are acceptable and, depending upon how they're written, somewhat compelling. Bottom line: Over the course of your career, you develop skills and grow professionally, explore different areas and make decisions. Your résumé should reflect that path.

Here are examples of stories you don't want your résumé to tell: "College communications grad who gets bored easily and bounces around from job to job at approximately one-year intervals." "Promising high-level administrative professional who lost her job and has been inexplicably unemployed for two and a half years." We'll cover how to avoid telling those stories shortly.

Résumé Rule #3 – A Résumé Should Be Easy to Digest.
Your résumé should be error-free, and free of overwritten descriptions and ornate language. It should have a little personality, but also be carefully edited so it is not redundant and does not contain a lot of extraneous information. The format should be tight, but not too tight, so it looks inviting at first glance and can be read without straining. There should be nothing about it that will stop me from quickly finding out about your background and how perfect you are for the job I'm filling (or, if not that job, another job I might fill in the near future, or a job I might hear about and pass your résumé along for).

RÉSUMÉ BASICS

The Length – It should be one page until it can't be, which shouldn't be less than five years into your professional career no matter how many internships or jobs you have had during school or since graduation. Take off class work and other school information as soon as you land your first job, unless whatever you did is impressive enough to sell you for your subsequent jobs. (Producing an award-winning short film IS impressive enough to make the cut. Taking an advanced film production class is not.)

The Format - Your résumé should be chronological unless you are making a career transition or have veered off your otherwise established career path. In those cases, your résumé should have a "Relevant Experience" section at the top, followed by an "Other Professional Experience" section. By doing this, you are making sure your most relevant job experience appears nearest the top.

> Your friends may know you as KatLovr18@gmail.com or Diamondznstilletoz@att.net, but these monikers are not suitable for business use. Plus, if I had to keep straight a bunch of "vanity plate" email addresses while dealing with multiple candidates for a single position, I'd never get the job filled. (Though I'll admit, I was kind of curious about what Diamondznstilletoz would wear to a job interview.)

The Look - Traditionally, résumés appeared in Times New Roman, but now that résumés are typically saved as a PDF (image) file, as long as it is one of the more popular fonts, you have more leeway. The Verdana, Cambia, and Calibri fonts in MS Word and comparable standard fonts on the Mac are perfectly acceptable and add a little more personality than Times New Roman.

NOTE: You will always create a PDF (or image) version of your résumé before you circulate it, so you don't have to worry about the font and formatting not transferring to the reader's computer.

ESSENTIAL ELEMENTS

Contact Information - Make sure your address is local. As I said above, a remote address on a submitted résumé will get that résumé set aside. If you don't yet live in the area where you are applying for a job, move first and then start your search. If I can't interview you in person and know that you are already living nearby, I won't consider you for a job that I am currently filling. What if you change your mind about moving or are delayed? Then I've wasted my valuable search time.

Education – As I mentioned above regarding length, until you have an industry job, you can include related class work, clubs, and other extracurricular activities. For your second job hunt – and the subsequent ones – you should keep only the information that is impressive and applicable to whatever job you are pursuing. Include your GPA next to your degree for finance, business, and legal & business affairs positions, or for all positions if your GPA is especially impressive. Move the education section to the bottom of your résumé when you have one post-graduate job under your belt or if you are applying for a first job with no connection to your degree; for instance, if you majored in Anthropology and are applying for a position in a TV network news division. Since your résumé is one page, the reader will see you have a college degree, but it doesn't need to be the first thing they see.

Professional Summary – This is a couple of sentences at the top of your résumé that describe your background and key skills as they relate to the job you are applying for. This is optional when you are a recent graduate, though in seeking an entry-level position where there might be 100 or more candidates, it usually can't hurt. When you have more extensive experience, though, or if you are making a career transition, it should be included as a way to introduce yourself and what you have to offer.

In the past, this block would've been called an "objective" and addressed what the candidate was seeking, not what he or she had to offer. If you are applying for a job that utilizes the skills and other aspects of your professional background that you most want to use going forward, your professional summary is an objective, even though it usually doesn't include the words "is seeking."

Examples of professional summaries:

Recent college graduate with degree in Broadcasting & Film obsessed with comedy and experienced in script copying and delivery, placing lunch orders and picking them up, and other intern duties that can be applied to an entry-level TV position.

Marketing major currently working in corporate marketing. Responsible for large research projects involving compiling and synthesizing focus group information and presenting results to senior management. Excellent written and oral communication skills, proactive, team player also able to work independently.

You'll also want to "answer" potential questions here, whether it's explaining away a gap in your résumé (in the first case) or indicating that you are making a transition (in both cases).

Penn graduate who took seven months off to care for a sick relative following brief local Production Assistant position. Recently relocated to Los Angeles to work in an on-set or office PA position in film or television. Dedicated, focused, driven. Looking forward to working hard and making a contribution to the success of a project.

Experienced event coordinator from prestigious financial corporation making a transition into entertainment. Oversaw events of all sizes, from intimate client dinners to holiday parties for several hundred guests. Adept at dealing with high-profile, high-net-worth individuals. Great multi-tasker, cool under pressure.

Note: Some of this content may also appear in your cover letter, but often hiring managers pop open your résumé first and if they see an unanswered question – or don't immediately connect to the candidate – they may not read the cover letter. The professional summary is insurance.

Experience – As indicated above in the "Basics" section, if your current/last position is not in the field you now want to be in and you have more relevant experience earlier in your career, include a section called "Relevant Experience" on top and a section called "Other Professional Experience" under that and sort your jobs accordingly. The idea is to make sure the recruiter or hiring executive sees the experience that sells you the best first. For new grads, this could be internship or volunteer experience.

Skills – If you are applying for a job where specific technical proficiency is required or desirable, list it. This includes editorial or IT positions and positions where tracking or other proprietary software is used. Do not include computer skills that are a "given," such as MS Office Suite or "Internet research," unless the job description specifies those skills and you do not have any work experience that would confirm your knowledge of them.

Other – This can include activities, awards or other recognition, or other special expertise or accomplishments and should be strategic. What you include should not only add personality to the résumé, but ideally also sell you in some way. For instance, having climbed Machu Picchu or competed on a reality cooking show not only makes you memorable on paper (and makes for a potentially interesting interview beyond job talk), but also shows dedication and follow-through.

References – I am generally not a fan of putting "References available upon request" at the bottom of the résumé. Of course you will provide references if asked! However, if your LinkedIn profile is complete and includes recommendations (more on that in Chapter 5), you should write, "See my LinkedIn profile for recommendations:" with a link, and then, "Additional references available upon request." That way, you are giving the reader an easy opportunity to see what other people have to say about you and indicating that this is not instead of providing references they can ask questions of, but in addition to them.

THE BIG DON'T

If you had an internship in the story department at Lionsgate, don't say it was a job as the assistant to the head of production. The entertainment industry is a small world, and there is a good possibility the person reading your résumé knows someone at Lionsgate and can check up on your tenure there. A lie like that will make you look stupid, especially since an internship at Lionsgate is already a good thing to have on your résumé and might've earned you an interview anyway. Even if you worked in the entertainment industry in another city, there is a chance the reader will know someone from that community (the industry is that interconnected), so it's best to just tell the real story.

 ACTION PROMPT 8

Create your own stellar entertainment résumé.

You probably already have a résumé. How do you know if it's stellar?

1) Is it visually appealing and easily absorbed by a recruiter or hiring executive? Have you used font size, bold type, italics, and spacing judiciously to move the eye down the page and draw attention to the key points on the page?

NOTE: I get asked a lot about creating a résumé that is scannable by an ATS system, the scanning software large employers use to weed out unqualified candidates. Allowing for circumstances where your résumé will be scanned is another reason to customize your résumé to the job you are applying for, but don't go overboard. If you write it for a human who is trying to fill a position you are actually qualified for, the machine should put you in the right pile without you having to flood your résumé with the same keywords many times.

2) If you are not an entry level candidate, does it include a professional summary that "sells" you for the job you want? Does it explain any gaps or other "question marks" on your resume?

3) Does your résumé depict career growth and development of professional skills even in situations where the job title is the same from one job to the next? In other words, is it written so that one job seems to lead to the next and so on, from the bottom (the chronological beginning) to the top?

4) Does each job description highlight all the duties and accomplishments from your previous jobs that promote you for the job you are seeking?

5) If you are at the beginning of your professional career, does it include non-industry jobs that demonstrate skills required by the job you are seeking? Server, customer service, and retail positions should all be included, especially if you don't have other positions that demonstrate ability to work with the public, and work under pressure, and the simple reliability that comes with having a job.

6) Is your résumé accurate, so that if one of your former employers, or internship or temp supervisors, got contacted (and they might, even if they aren't listed as references), they would confirm what you put on your résumé?

7) Is your résumé written consistently (the same date format for every job, everything indented the same amount, etc.) and free of typos and errors?
This is CRUCIAL. It can make or break you getting called in, even if you are the most qualified candidate. Sloppiness/carelessness usually gets you a trip to the "no" pile. Have someone else proofread your job hunt materials before you send them out. When they give them the okay, have someone else proofread them, too.

Stefanie Wallace

310-555-1773   StefanieWallace13@gmail.com

EDUCATION

Boston University College of Communication
Bachelor of Science in Public Relations, May 2013
> Boston University Los Angeles Internship Programs: Advertising & PR Track, Fall 2012

INDUSTRY-RELATED EXPERIENCE

College Media Corp (Boston)   January - May 2013
Marketing & Advertising Intern
- Contributed to and maintained online advertising decks for client accounts.
- Created media lists with ideas for college audience growth tailored to specific clients.
- Tracked and provided analysis of daily and monthly website traffic in Google Analytics with specific strategies to improve numbers.

The Franklin Talent Agency (Los Angeles)   September – December 2012
Comedy Department Intern
- Maintained agency website's comedy roster by adding new and updated client biographies, head shots, video clips, and contact information.
- Followed up with club owners regarding ticket sales, total gross, etc., for client appearances.
- Covered phones for department Vice President and other desks when assistants were away.
- Distributed contracts, deal memo, and other Business Affairs paperwork to agents, clients, and managers.
- Performed miscellaneous office tasks as needed, such as filing, photocopying, and errands.

The American Pavilion, Cannes International Film Festival   May 2012
Talent Intern
- Escorted judges, actors, and other VIPs to screenings and receptions.
- Assisted festival's production team with interviews, event coverage, and other electronic press kit shoots.

WBUR (Boston)   January – May 2012
Events Intern
- Updated categorized contact lists for different types of special events.
- Entered guest lists for each event into electronic invitation service.
- Provided onsite assistance to event VP and her staff.

ADDITIONAL EXPERIENCE

TGI Fridays (Indianapolis, IN)   Summers, 2010 – 2013
Hostess
- Award-winning* greeter and seater of guests in the busy downtown location.
- Star of regional training video and onsite trainer for other hosts in four local locations.

*Award given by manager and other staff members who were impressed by my tirelessness and relentless cheerfulness and ability to put a smile on the face of even the most otherwise surly customer.

CHAPTER 11
WINNING ENTERTAINMENT COVER LETTERS

As I said in the last chapter, your job hunt materials speak for you. If the résumé is an ad for you in a particular position, the cover letter is a firm handshake and introductory spiel before the big pitch. Answer the questions: *What position am I interested in and why? What are the most relevant and compelling reasons you should take a look at my résumé and consider my candidacy?*

RULES FOR WINNING COVER LETTERS

Cover Letter Rule #1 - Share Your Hopes and Dreams Only if They Sell You for the Job.
Do not tell me you love animals unless I am hiring a horse trainer or dog groomer. You can tell me you've wanted to work in the film industry since you were five, but if you back that up by saying that in high school you recreated the original *Star Wars* trilogy in a series of claymation short films, then I know you really mean it and you back up your passion with action. I might even say, "Wow." I might also be intrigued enough to interview you even if you aren't a great match for the job.

Cover Letter Rule #2 - Personalize Your Letter for Each Submission.
This customization shows the kind of attention to detail and work ethic I want from someone I am considering hiring. (In other words, you've already impressed me in the first sentence of your cover letter! Congratulations!)

Cover Letter Rule #3 - Don't Regurgitate Your Résumé.
I want to know some basics about your background and how you qualify for the position I am filling. Stick to identifying your most current position (or situation, if you are just coming out of school) and sharing the most pertinent things about your background as they relate to this particular job.

Cover Letter Rule #4 - Bring "You" to the Page.
If there is something unique about you, please tell me. I read dozens of cover letters for each position I fill. If you can add a little extra something, such as

telling me that your great-grandfather played opposite Douglas Fairbanks, Jr. in a pirate movie, you just woke me up (thanks!) and made yourself memorable. If you got second-runner-up in the "Most Beautiful Baby of Hartford, Connecticut" contest when you were six months old and you can somehow artfully work that into the letter (maybe tell me that not winning taught you perseverance or humility), do so. As I said about the claymation filmmaker in #1, even if you are slightly wrong for the job, I might invite you in for an interview because you jolted me out of my fog and I can probably count on an interesting conversation when I meet you.

Cover Letter Rule #5 – Explain Away Red Flags on Your Résumé if You Can.
As with your professional summary, you should take the opportunity in your cover letter to explain away a gap after college (for caring for an elderly relative or touring Europe, for instance) or being in your last three jobs a short time, if it was through no fault of your own (if the companies downsized or folded, or your boss left the company). But if there is a bigger story, such as being fired or quitting after only a few months at a company because you were asked to do something you didn't think was ethical, or because your boss was abusive, don't mention that. Instead indicate that you are looking for a stable position you can grow in and leave it at that. Explanations of tricky job transitions are best left until the interview – and even then must be treated carefully. (See the interview chapter in Phase Three for details on handling this.)

COVER LETTER BASICS
Length – Three-quarters to one page tops. Tell me only enough to entice me to look at your résumé.

Format – In most cases, a formal business letter is best, as an attachment, especially for an office position. Formal business letters are a rare form of communication outside the legal & business affairs department, but I like to know you CAN create one if needed, and that you have gone to the trouble to do so in order to submit yourself for the job. For on-set positions, you can be more informal. In the body of the email, indicate what position you are seeking, who you know on the production (or how you heard about the opportunity), and your relevant experience.

Font – In an attached letter, it should match your résumé font. In an email, any basic font will do.

ESSENTIAL ELEMENTS

Paragraph 1 - As indicated in Winning Cover Letter Rule #2, personalizing each letter is vital. Open by identifying the job you are submitting yourself for and how you heard about it. If someone referred you for the job, mention him or her by name here. Follow that with one sentence about why you are interested and/or the right person to hire. (Example: "I am writing to express my interest in the assistant job you have available at Pixar. I was told about this opportunity by Ann Morris in your finance department. I have seen every Pixar movie, even the shorts, and can quote most of them from memory, so working within your organization would be amazing to me.")

Paragraph 2 - Include the most impressive and/or relevant experience you have had. It doesn't matter if it's paid or unpaid if it shows you can do the job. If you raised financing and produced a $30,000 short film while in college, tell me that. If you volunteered on a student short that shot nights in the dead of winter in Minnesota and loved every second of the experience, tell me that. Working the door at a prestigious event with many VIP attendees and managing to avoid making anyone mad or admitting any gate crashers counts. It shouldn't be the only thing you include, but for certain positions, such as working for high-level industry professionals or for those who deal with celebrities and other bigwigs, that shows the all-important ability to finesse delicate situations.

Paragraph 3 - This paragraph may or may not be necessary when you are starting out. Let's say you've dedicated the second paragraph to your internship or relevant job experience. This paragraph can include work-study experience, school activities (being the event coordinator for your fraternity and what that entailed, for instance), volunteer work, or non-entertainment jobs you had in school. (Yes, as I said in the résumé chapter, having a retail or food service job during summers or even part-time during the school year should be mentioned. You work hard. Tell me.)

The Big Wrap-up - This should be basic. Thank me for my time and consideration. Tell me how much you appreciate being considered for the job and how much you would enjoy coming in for an interview. Make sure you tell me how to reach you, especially in a formal cover letter. If you've followed all the instructions in this chapter, after reading your cover letter, I'll likely already be interested in meeting you, even before I dive into your equally impressive résumé.

GETTING CREATIVE

Years ago, I opened up a flat envelope at my office and pulled out a small stack of pages, on the top of which was one that shouted in a large font written across the page:

"Andrew Paskoff is coming to Tinseltown!"

Job candidates had tried the "clever-to-get-your-attention" ploy many times before, but this one immediately made me smile. Under the headline was a mock interview with the candidate about why he was coming out. It was polite, sincere, well written, and genuinely funny. Underneath this page were a traditional cover letter and a résumé. I scanned those pages and immediately wanted to hire (not just meet with but HIRE) this guy. Why?

1) His creativity was not flippant, braggy, or otherwise a turn-off.

2) He broke the rules and also followed the rules, with his real (winning) cover letter and (stellar) résumé included in the mailing.

In summary, he came across as a sweet, hard-working, funny, but probably somewhat low-key guy who would be a pleasure to have around and would do his job well. I contacted him and met with him when he arrived in, er, Tinseltown. He was exactly as his materials suggested. Unfortunately, someone else who had been impressed by his mailing snatched him up before I had the right opening for him. (That's right; others were also eager to get him on their teams.)

Note: I reconnected with him not long ago and interviewed him for Your Industry Insider. His career path lived up to the promise he had shown early on, and it was a pleasure to share his story with my readers: http://yourindustryinsider.com/2013/04/andrew-paskoff/.

ADDITIONAL MATERIALS

If you are asked to include specific writing samples, make sure you follow instructions to the letter and get help if you need it. For instance, PR jobs often require sample press releases. Don't dig up something you did in class and think, "It's not great, but it'll do." Create new ones if you need to and then have your most PR-savvy friends read and critique them.

There might be other examples of your work that you should mention in your cover letter. If you've been writing the company newsletter at your receptionist job, for instance, say that, and then bring a copy to the interview. Make sure whatever you're showing doesn't violate your company's confidentiality policy, though. That shows a lack of common sense and/or consideration and would make you look bad to your potential employer.

 # ACTION PROMPT 9

Compose your winning entertainment cover letter.

Here are the questions you need to answer to know if your cover letter is winning:

1) Have you created a first paragraph that allows you to indicate what job you are applying for and why you think you would be a good fit? This is a section that identifies you and why you are interested in a specific job, so you'll want to add the specifics for each job you apply for.

2) Does your second paragraph include the most relevant or compelling reason for hiring you for your target job? If you can't think of what should be here, read the job descriptions for your target job and figure out what the core requirements are. Find some experience in your background that relates to the core experience – even, as I said, if it was not an entertainment industry position, or a paid position for that matter. You are basically saying, "Here's how you know I can do the job" with this paragraph.

3) Does your third paragraph (if you have one) flesh out the rest of your experience, especially as it relates to the qualifications of your target job?

4) Does your big wrap-up include your contact information and indicate gratitude and eagerness to move forward in the process of getting the job?

5) Is your letter free of grammatical and spelling errors, and other typos? Since you will be customizing at least the top paragraph of your letter, you will want to have it proofread by multiple people each time you send it out. As I think I have made clear, errors in your job hunt materials can cost you the interview – and with it, the opportunity to get hired for the job.

Stefanie Wallace

310-555-1773   StefanieWallace13@gmail.com

Hiring Executive
Mystic Public Relations
6555 Sunset Boulevard
Los Angeles, CA 90028

September 13, 2013

Dear Hiring Executive,

I am contacting you in response to your posting on Linked In for a Receptionist/Administrative Assistant. Although I am a recent college graduate seeking an entry-level position, I have had a lot of experience in Public Relations through my internships, in addition to the coursework I completed as part of my Public Relations degree from Boston University.

I have had experience interacting with talent and other high-level individuals, including covering phones in the comedy department at The Franklin Talent Agency and working events for WBUR. I also spent a memorable month in Cannes in 2012 escorting talent and other VIPs around the film festival and providing support during interviews for the festival's electronic press kit. Lastly, I spent four summers, including this past summer, being the best TGI Fridays hostess in the history of the franchise. Or trying my best to be, anyway.

In addition to my work dealing with people directly, I also gained quite a bit of administrative experience during my internships, including internet research, compiling media lists, updating databases and websites, sending electronic event invitations, as well as filing, photocopying, and helping assemble presentation decks.

In summary, I would love to be a part of your organization and I hope that after reviewing my resume, you'll consider having me in to discuss my qualifications further.

Sincerely,

CHAPTER 12
THE WEB'S ROLE IN YOUR CAREER

In this chapter, you are creating an online identity that will help you land your target entertainment job and/or advance your dream pursuit. If you used the previous two chapters to create a stellar résumé and winning cover letter respectively, you are already in good shape. What you will be doing here is applying that content to the various places where your professional identity will live and grow on the web. But let's start with a little tidying up, okay?

CLEANING THE SLATE

If you are ready to get serious about your entertainment dreams, you want your online presence to reflect that and portray you in a way that will give you an advantage as you launch and grow your career. I cannot tell you how many times I have either Googled a job candidate and found something that made me rethink him or her, or had an executive veto a candidate I have approved because the executive found something on the Internet about the candidate.

The entertainment industry is a high-stakes business, and you don't want to be passed up for a job or other opportunity because your Internet presence did not reflect your professional best.

BUILDING YOUR PROFESSIONAL WEB PRESENCE

Below, we will break down each of the sites commonly used for professional networking, starting with the number-one career-oriented social networking site on the web.

LINKEDIN

In almost all cases, LinkedIn is the most important place for you as an entertainment professional to be. The only exceptions are if you work exclusively on set or are a performer (actor, singer, standup comic) without a day job or with a day job (such as bartending or babysitting) that does not involve office work. Otherwise, LinkedIn will be the home base for your online professional identity and the main place where you will connect with others in the industry.

Your profile is an online version of your résumé, but with a more personal twist. The summary at the top of your LinkedIn profile page should be written as a professional mission statement crossed with a focused career bio. Some people like to write it in the first person, but regardless of whether it's in the first person or third person, it should be well-written and compelling. Before you write yours, you should look at other people's profiles on LinkedIn and find a few that make you want to work with the people they're about. Those are the ones you should model yours after, as they reflect your personal style and values.

Reaching Out
There are job hunt tools through LinkedIn that make it advantageous to connect to your real-world contacts on LinkedIn; so take out your "who do you know?" list and make sure everyone on it who is on LinkedIn is a connection of yours – and while you're at it, make sure your entertainment-related LinkedIn connections are all on your "who do you know?" list.

Beyond that, you should know that some LinkedIn users connect only with people they have met in person or done business with. Others try to connect with as many people as possible regardless of who they are. I'm right in the middle on this. I connect with people who are in entertainment and/or have some connection to my professional life, whether I have met them or not. I would recommend you adopt a similar strategy. As we move into using LinkedIn for job hunting, you'll see why it is helpful to connect with people you do not know who are in your field.

NOTE: If someone takes the time to add a personal note to their request to connect with me, I usually connect with them more automatically than someone who just sends the request with the default language and leaves me to figure out why I might want to connect with them.

Getting Recommendations
Recommendations on LinkedIn are positive reviews of your work from former professors, employers, bosses, clients, and even co-workers, and they are a must when you are job-seeking and/or starting to establish your professional reputation. Once you have your profile set up and polished, and have started connecting with your network, you'll want to reach out for recommendations.

LinkedIn Groups
These are groups set up by users to allow discussions and sharing of resources

centered upon some commonality. There are many groups on LinkedIn, including college alumni groups (both run by the school administration and created by alumni) and groups for specific fields, positions, or interests (entertainment professionals, recruiters, self-publishing).

You will periodically get group recommendations from LinkedIn on the right-hand side of your homepage based on the content of your profile. Also, you will see in your feed when one of your connections joins a group or posts a discussion within one of the groups. If you don't see the group you want and think others would find it useful, you can easily start your own.

Job Recommendations from LinkedIn
LinkedIn has a great feature called "Jobs You Might Be Interested In." It's a weekly email based on keywords from your profile, groups you join, and other data collected through your use of the site. You can also search the LinkedIn job postings, and in some groups, members post open positions they hear about.

The Bottom Line on LinkedIn
LinkedIn marries traditional job search tools with social networking in ways that can, if used properly, give you a professional leg up. It's important, though, to take the time to make sure your presence there is polished and up-to-date and that you are being proactive in networking.

FACEBOOK
Facebook is a flexible social media platform and one that people use for different reasons. Some keep it entirely personal, choosing to interact only with their real-life friends. If that is the case with you, take a moment to go to your privacy settings and make sure only your friends can see the content you post, as well as any pictures or comments that are posted when you are tagged. If you and your friends like to share party pictures or anything else that could turn off a potential employer or collaborator, be vigilant in staying up-to-date on privacy settings.

However, before you decide to keep Facebook exclusively for personal interaction, consider that the main users of Facebook are those in their mid-thirties and up, as well as businesses and other organizations that are vying for your business or attention. In other words, it is a good place to network virtually with people who are further along in their entertainment career than you are and/or part of organizations you might want to work with or for at some point.

Facebook is usually the career home base for people in production (costumers, composers, etc.) and for performers. Entrepreneurs often also maintain professional presences on Facebook. For others, it's primarily social and a secondary place to talk about work and to connect professionally.

The Bottom Line on Facebook
Facebook is a more casual atmosphere to establish a professional identity and connection than LinkedIn, but you want to make sure you are presenting your best self to get the most out of your time there.

TWITTER
If you are unfamiliar with Twitter, here's the gist: People interact on it in 140-character-or-less posts on all kinds of topics, from pop culture to politics to business. They use hashtags (words or phrases preceded by the # symbol, such as #POTUS or #Oscars) to label the topic of certain posts so people can find out what topics are trending and search by that topic to hear what people are saying about it.

Twitter can be a good place to make your presence known and, in some cases, interact directly with individuals and organizations that could help your entertainment career.

The Bottom Line on Twitter
Twitter is not a "must" unless you have a defined objective for using it. Your identity there is limited (one photo and 140 characters max of text on your profile page); unless you put in time to interact and build relationships, you will not get much return.

Blogs/Personal Websites
How about having your own domain, an online place where you can house your reel and otherwise highlight your work or expound on your passion or profession? When done right, it's an excellent platform on which to develop your career or business and/or grow your reputation.

Most, if not all, entertainment professionals who need to show their work to potential employers, such as editors, actors, directors, and composers, have websites dedicated to housing their reels. The key for these "showcase" sites is to keep them focused and simple. Highlight the work that you are most proud of and that most represents what you want to do in the future. If you need to, shoot something on your own or work for free to get the right material. It is no longer frowned upon to have "amateur" material included on your professional reel; the line between amateur and professional has blurred as the Internet has gained popularity as a content distributor. Good is good, whether you were paid for it or not.

Depending upon your entertainment pursuit, you may also want a site that goes beyond being a showcase for your work. A website can be an expression of your passion or expertise, which can establish or enhance your entertainment reputation (aka brand) and sometimes facilitate contact with established industry pros. Chicago-area native Danny King started his film criticism blog, The King Bulletin (http://www.thekingbulletin.com/), while in high school because he loved seeing films and thinking and writing about them. Because of his blog, he got invited to some Chicago press screenings. And though he cannot say for sure, he believes the blog, as proof of his passion for film and his critical thinking skills, contributed to his admission to certain schools, including the one he chose to attend, New York University.

Playbills vs. Paying Bills (http://www.playbillsvspayingbills.com/) was created by actor Ben Whitehair and two of his acting school friends when they fanned out to Los Angeles, Chicago, and New York, respectively, to launch their careers. The website was a resource for actors, providing interviews with agents, casting directors, and other industry pros and providing first-person accounts of life in the audition trenches. Though it is not very active anymore, the site definitely established their identities as actors, gave them an excuse to reach out to established talent representatives (besides just submitting themselves as potential clients), and got them publicity for their careers. (Your Industry Iinsider spotlighted the site in September 2010.)

ACTION PROMPT 10

Construct your pristine, professional web presence.

1) Clean the Slate

Part One – Tidy up your own web presence.

You're probably on Facebook, Twitter, or other social networking sites. First look at your own profile, and at your photos and notes. Anything that could be viewed negatively should be removed. Even if it was a joke, if an outsider reading a comment or looking at a picture could get the wrong idea, it's better to take it off.

Now look on your wall for photos and other content your friends have tagged you in. Un-tag anything that is questionable, and check for tags regularly going forward, especially if your friends believe something didn't happen unless it's all over the web. (Good news! If you un-tag yourself from a photo or post, you cannot be retagged, so you only have to un-tag each photo once.)

Do this "home base" and outreach cleaning for every site on which you have a presence. If your Twitter feed has ongoing rude or obscene replies from your friends to everything you say, you might consider trying to clean up your Twitter communications. You wouldn't have that kind of back and forth at an entertainment-industry networking event. Having it on Twitter has the potential to do the same level (or greater) damage to your career prospects.

Part Two – Look for potential problems on other sites.

What comes up when you search for your own name? Is there anything you wouldn't want a potential employer to see, such as an angry comment on someone else's blog post? If you can get it off the web, do so. If you can't get it off the web, don't panic. Creating career-friendly web content is the objective of the rest of this chapter, so whatever you wish you could erase will naturally move down the search results as more of your positive content is added.

2) Build Your Professional Web Presence
LinkedIn
Here are the steps to creating a top-notch LinkedIn profile:

Choose an appropriate Professional Headline. Some people use their job title, such as Casting Director. Others use their field and a generic designation, such as Marketing Professional, especially when they are between jobs or transitioning within their field. If you are doing more than one thing, such as writing scripts on the side while you are an executive assistant, assuming it won't cause a problem with your employer, you can put something like "Administrative Professional and Freelance Writer" as your heading.

Create your Professional Summary. Combining elements from the headline block at the top of your résumé, if you have one, and your cover letter, craft a short, first-person professional bio that highlights the experience and skills you have that are most relevant to the path you are on or the path you want to be on. If you are pursuing two different jobs, such as working at a film studio and working on a set, you'll need to highlight the experience and skills that apply to both. Make sure that a potential employer looking at your LinkedIn page won't be confused.

Import the experience part of your résumé either by uploading it or cutting and pasting it into the provided fields. LinkedIn sorts jobs chronologically and does not allow you to do sections for "Related Experience" and "Other Professional Experience." I recommend you include full details of the jobs related to what you are currently pursuing, and edit or omit much of the detail on the other jobs. That way, someone scanning your profile will be able to tell what you are focused on since it takes up more real estate on the page.

Select and upload your LinkedIn photo. It should be of your whole head from the shoulders or base of the neck up, and you should be looking at the camera. Make sure the lighting is good, your attire and the setting are professional or neutral, and that you are smiling.

Connecting
How do you connect? On LinkedIn, you send an invitation to people you are interested in connecting with. LinkedIn makes you indicate how

you know the person you are reaching out to and then pre-populates the message field with "I'd like to add you to my professional network on LinkedIn." If you are sending the invitation to someone you don't know, you should briefly personalize your request. It's fine to add, "We met at the entertainment panel you spoke at last week. I am the guy who asked about residuals," or "I read your blog often and love your ideas on viral marketing in the industry."

Who do you connect with? Start with your real-life network: Your friends and their friends, classmates and professors, your internship coordinators, people you temped with, etc. Beyond that, LinkedIn will suggest people you might know, and/or you can allow LinkedIn to run an app to check your contacts for people on LinkedIn. You'll be surprised how quickly your connections add up. And then any time you meet someone in person or online, take a moment to connect with him or her on LinkedIn. It's a good way to keep track of contacts and build your LinkedIn network at the same time.

Recommendations
Go to the "Recommendations" section via the profile drop-down menu and choose "Request Recommendation." Include a message that asks the recipient to recommend your work and thanks the person for his or her time. LinkedIn allows you to review recommendations before they go up on your profile, so if you don't see what you were hoping for when you get the draft, you can politely ask the person to address those specifics.

Facebook
Getting Started. Creating a basic Facebook page is pretty easy. If you don't have a Facebook page, set one up and keep your career objectives in mind while you are using the site.

Ways to interact once your profile is ready:
Use your wall to post about your work life or school projects you are doing. Though it may feel contrived at first, your work life (which in your case may currently mean school) is part of who you are and will become more of a focus as you mature, especially if you have big goals. It can't hurt to start getting the word out about how you are moving toward those goals. You never know who might reach out to provide you with a valuable resource or connection.

You have the ability to keep some posts viewable by friends only and to allow some to be seen by the public. It may take some effort to get the hang of this, but it's a good feature to know about if you want to publicize your work, yet at the same time you have a photogenic dog that looks good in hats but whose photos you don't want the world to see.

Friend people you have met through internships, work, or other professional interactions. This is pretty self-explanatory.

Subscribe to the posts of public people who allow this. This is a good way to keep track of what business leaders and other public figures are up to – and to hear about it "from the horse's mouth," as they say.

"Like" your college and alumni Facebook pages and other groups relevant to what you are doing or want to do. There are all kinds of pages on Facebook. Your Industry Insider has a page (which you should definitely like). There are also pages called "Casting Notices" and "Staff Me Up," with offshoots specific to other cities or regions. Many businesses and public people (actors and others who seek an audience) have pages. "Like" the pages of people, organizations, businesses, causes, and other entities that appeal to you or that could be helpful to your career.

Join groups. Whereas the primary objective for a page is for the administrator(s) to share information, a group is for interaction and sharing resources among members. Some groups are open (anyone can join), some are closed (administrators approve membership), and some are secret (only the members know the group exists). Join groups that appeal to you or that could help you with your career.

Spend a little time interacting on pages and in groups. Comment on posts on Your Industry Insider's wall, on other pages you have liked, and in groups you are a member of. Also, respond to other people's comments. If the page allows users to post, you can put up a link that is relevant to the users or ask a smart question. Always be thoughtful and diplomatic. Establish yourself by sharing your interests, knowledge, and expertise. It's like networking you would do in person, but you can do it without leaving home – and while wearing your pajamas.

Twitter

Getting Started

Pick your Twitter handle. I decided on @ShowBizInfo when setting up the feed for Your Industry Insider, because anyone can tell what it is and follow me based on whether they are interested in showbiz info. If you already have an established entertainment career goal or passion, you could incorporate it into your Twitter handle. For instance, if you are an aspiring actor, use @StefThesp or @StefanieActs. If you are starting out in marketing, you could use something like @MktgWhiz3.

Create your profile. It's a simple page comprising a photo or logo that will appear alongside your tweets and a simple 140-character (or less) description of yourself or your organization. Be clever if you want, but make sure you are clear.

Ways to interact once your profile is ready:

Follow some people. Follow people you know or who share your interests, businesses you patronize or want to possibly work for, celebrities you admire, etc. Once you start following people, you will get suggestions from Twitter about more people to follow, but you definitely want to seek out the right connections for your career aspirations.

Example: Let's say you want to intern or work at The Ellen DeGeneres Show. You can follow the show's feed, Ellen's feed, and the feeds of others associated with the show. (Search by using the show's hashtag to figure out which staff members have their own feed.) Comment on the show's content using that hashtag, retweet whatever they say to your followers, and once you have established yourself as a fan and made some clever comments that demonstrate how smart you are, eventually you can reach out and ask them about working there. They may just tell you to go to the job board for the show, but they may give you inside scoop, especially if you are seeking an unpaid college internship.

CHAPTER 13
YOUR ENTERTAINMENT CAREER PITCH

It's a fast-paced world, and you never know who might be able to help you. A chance meeting with a stranger might lead to the opportunity of a lifetime – or even just a little help reaching the next step on your career path. The trick is being ready at all times to quickly and succinctly explain what you do and/or what you want to do and what you need in order to move forward.

That's where your pitch comes in. You will use it on the fly in person and on the phone, as well as in email and other written communications. You might even boil it down to a text message or Twitter blast. Though the actual content you use will vary depending upon the context, your pitch is a short spiel that tells who you are, what you do, what you want to do, and/or what you need. You already use some version of your pitch in your daily life. "I'm Sarah Johnson. I'm a Film and Television major, and I'm trying to get into your Film Production class," you might say to a professor. It comes off so naturally that you don't even think of it as a pitch – but it is.

So what would be the entertainment-career version of Sarah's pitch? Let's say she has graduated and needs a job. "I'm Sarah Johnson. I just graduated from the University of Florida's Film & Television program, and I'm looking for a Production Assistant job" is acceptable, but if you have applicable experience that might give you an advantage, you want to add that: "I'm Sarah Johnson. I just graduated from the University of Florida Film & Television program. I worked on more than twenty student projects, as well as wrote, produced, and directed two short films of my own and interned on set for a commercial production house. I'm looking for a Production Assistant job."

From the first version to the second, you went from being a promising candidate for an on-set Production Assistant job to being a fully qualified, experienced candidate for a Production Assistant job. And even if the person you are speaking with (or sending an email to) cannot get you a PA job, presenting yourself as hardworking and experienced never hurts.

Sarah has a straightforward pitch. She wants one thing and needs one pitch. But what if you have your day job needs and your dream pursuit, or are following parallel career paths? For instance, Roger has been a runner for a TV production company for a year now and is sick of driving around L.A. all day. Since he wants to be a TV writer, he believes working a desk job at a TV-related company would give him an opportunity to network that he isn't getting now. He also wants an agent or manager who can shop his scripts and get him meetings at the shows he wants to write for.

Roger is picking up a script at a major talent agency. As he passes through the lobby and sees all the busy Hollywood movers and shakers, he feels intimidated but intrigued. He wonders what it would be like to work there. He gets into the elevator and presses the button for the top floor. As he's thinking about that, the elevator stops on the way up and a suited man gets in. He looks at Roger quizzically and says, "Hi, I'm Bob. Do you work here?"

Roger could say, "Hi," and look at his shoes. In which case, he should give himself an F for networking. But Roger is shy and is caught off guard by the question. With a little more effort, he could blurt out, "Hi, I'm Roger. I'm delivering a script from my company." That would give him a C since he has provided only basics and given Bob no reason to communicate further.

Roger might be torn, though. He's in one of the most prestigious agencies in the world. He was just thinking about how he'd love to work there, but on the other hand, he also needs representation. Which version of his pitch should he use: The aspiring writer pitch or the entertainment worker bee pitch? He quickly decides that since he's still polishing his writing samples and this agency doesn't typically represent new writers, he should go with his worker bee pitch – with one addition.

He says, "Hi, I'm Roger Perkins. I graduated from Rutgers last year, and I'm an aspiring TV writer. I'm a runner picking up a script for Imagine, but I've always thought it would be cool to work at an agency. Do you work here?" (It sounds like a mouthful, but once you are used to saying it, it will come out naturally.) Roger has provided basic information, expressed interest in working at an agency, and asked a question, continuing the conversation and giving Bob an opening to tell him more about himself. And he has mentioned his dream pursuit. Well done. A+.

What Roger wants from Bob in this case is some information on working within an agency and maybe even a referral to someone who can help him get a job at the company. Bob may even know of an opening. On the other hand, he may not even work at the agency. But since he's used his full pitch, Roger is likely to find out one way or another. On the other hand, if he'd fallen silent or just given the bare minimum of information, he would have had no way of knowing if he missed his big chance.

Crafting your entertainment career pitch is not something you can typically do on the fly when you need it. It's something you should prepare in advance, giving it thought and trying it out loud to make sure you don't trip over your words. If it feels awkward or silly, you need to get past that. This is an important tool for your entertainment career and could be the difference between getting a big opportunity and spending a silent elevator ride staring at your shoes.

ACTION PROMPT 11

Craft your concise, engaging entertainment career pitch.

Now it's time to craft your pitch. Start with your objective – what you will be using your pitch to get. Like Roger, you should focus first on your job or day job aspirations when crafting your pitch. (Supporting yourself financially is your number-one job in the entertainment industry, even if you ultimately want to be a sitcom actress or screenwriter.)

What job do you want? (Or, if you are all set jobwise, what's your goal?) If you want more than one job, that's okay. You can say you are looking for "either a PA job or an assistant job" with no problem. However, "I want to work in television" is too vague. Even if you don't care what you do, "I want to work in television" doesn't tell someone whether you are inexperienced and on a particular path or an entry-level candidate. It's too vague. "I am looking for an entry-level position in television" is okay, but "I am looking for a Production Assistant or assistant job in television" is best. You want to prompt them to think of some way they can help you, if it's a chance meeting, or know exactly what you are looking for, if your résumé is circulating around town with a brief email to introduce you.

What is the most basic way to identify you? Are you "a recent NYU grad" or "a graduate of the University of Arizona who is transitioning from marketing in the pharmaceutical industry into entertainment marketing"? It just has to tell the person you are talking/writing to the minimum amount of information he or he needs in order to know who you are.

How can you sell yourself for whatever your goal is? If you graduated from an entertainment program, especially if it was at a top school, your identifier already sells you a little. But you want to add one more sentence if you have it: "I interned as a PA at Conan for a semester while I was in school," or "I've been temping in the talent department at HBO, but they don't have anything permanent available right now." Use anything that tells them you can do the job.

Now practice, practice, practice. Once you have your pitch composed, practice a verbal version of it. You don't want the first time it comes out of your mouth to be when you are meeting a studio HR executive at a networking event.

READYING YOUR RESOURCES CHECKLIST

Review of Phase Two

ACTION PROMPT 6

___ You completed your *Knowledge* list.

___ You completed your *Expertise* list.

___ You completed your *Cash* list.

___ You completed your *Talent* list.

ACTION PROMPT 7

___ You made a list: "Who do you know (and how do you know them)?"

___ You gave at least a little thought to what you can do for them.

ACTION PROMPT 8

___ Your résumé is visually appealing and scannable by a recruiter or hiring executive.

___ Your résumé includes a professional summary at the top that "sells" you for the job you want and explains away any gaps or other "question marks" on your résumé.

___ Your résumé depicts career growth and development of professional skills even in situations where the job title is the same from one job to the next.

___ Your résumé contains job descriptions that highlight all the duties and accomplishments from your previous jobs that promote you for the job you are seeking.

___ Your résumé includes non-industry jobs that demonstrate skills required by the job you are seeking, assuming you are at or near the beginning of your professional career.

___ Your résumé is accurate, so that if one of your former employers, or internship or temp supervisors, were contacted, they would confirm what you put on your résumé.

___ Your résumé is written consistently (the same date format for every job, everything indented the same amount, etc.) and free of typos and errors.

ACTION PROMPT 9

____ You created a first paragraph that allows you to indicate what job you are applying for and why you think you would be a good fit.

____ Your second paragraph includes the most relevant or compelling reason someone would have for hiring you for your target job.

____ Your third paragraph (if you have one) fleshes out the rest of your experience, especially as it relates to the qualifications of your target job.

____ Your big wrap-up includes your contact information and indicates gratitude and eagerness to move forward in the process of getting the job.

____ Your letter is free of grammatical and spelling errors, and other typos.

ACTION PROMPT 10

____ You tidied up your own web presence, including checking posts, photos, and notes on sites where you might have existing profiles, such as Facebook and Twitter.

____ You looked for potential problems on other sites by doing Internet searches. You built a professional web presence on:

____ LinkedIn (including getting recommendations and connecting with others)

____ Facebook (including friending professional contacts, joining groups and liking pages, and spending some time interacting in a career-focused way)

____ Twitter (including research and following organizations and people who could be helpful for your career)

ACTION PROMPT 11

You crafted a pitch (or multiple pitches for multiple goals, starting with the one that will help you support yourself financially, especially if you are pursuing a "dream job") comprising three elements:

____ What job do you want (or what other goal are you seeking)?

____ Who are you (described in a very basic way)?

____ What tidbit of information best promotes you for your goal?

____ You have practiced your pitch so that it sounds natural to you.

PHASE THREE: GETTING IN THE GAME

In Phase One, you identified your current entertainment career goals and delved into the motivations behind those goals. The objective was to home in on what success would look like for you beyond a job title or specific achievement. You also thought about first steps up the ladder for a career job or compatible day jobs (and even potential parallel careers) to support your dream pursuit.

In Phase Two, you learned about Hollywood currency, considered what kind of currency you already possess, and evaluated how you could accrue more of all kinds. You created a stellar résumé (or multiple stellar résumés) and a winning cover letter template you could customize for each job submission. You then took what you had done with those documents and applied the necessary elements to creating a career-forward web presence. And lastly, you crafted a pitch or pitches for yourself, which you could use as needed in written and verbal communication.

Phase Three is all about taking those tools you created in Phase Two, going out, finding the right opportunities, and getting a job that will establish and support you as an entertainment professional working toward your ultimate vision of success.

CHAPTER 14
ACTIVATING YOUR NETWORK

Back when *Criminal Minds* First Assistant Director (AD) Ian Woolf was applying for the DGA trainee program for becoming an AD, he reached out to his sister's friend, who had been through the application process, in order to get insider information on what would be on the infamously challenging test and any other tips that could give him an advantage. *Captain America* screenwriter Christopher Markus got his entertainment day job at a Warner Bros.–based film production company through a friend of a friend. These are just two examples from Your Industry Insider profile subjects who were able to use their networks to get what they needed at the time.

Take out your entertainment networking list. With any luck, you've spent time fleshing it out. Regardless, look at it again and think about who might be missing. As I said before, you will not be required to contact everyone on the list now, but put everyone you can think of on it, including second-degree connections. Even people you don't know could end up being helpful in your career. For instance, if your music editor brother-in-law works on Ben Stiller's movies, put Ben Stiller on the list. Someday you might want to work for his company or on one of his projects. Your brother-in-law could provide an "in."

The bottom line for this process is that you never know when someone you don't know well might become more significant as you pursue new opportunities down the line. If they're not on the list, you might forget about them and miss an opportunity to get that much closer to your goal.

KEEPING TRACK OF YOUR NETWORK

As you start using your entertainment networking list to move forward with your career, you'll want to create a related Network Tracking Sheet to have a record of who you reached out to, why and how, and what happened. This will be your go-to place for information on communication with industry contacts, including referrals they give you and follow-up you must do. It is a tool you can use for your initial job hunt, subsequent job hunts, and other entertainment goals (getting a manager, making a short film, booking your band at a particular club, etc.) and it's up to you to make it as comprehensive as possible. Remember, relationships are high-value currency in entertainment.

RECONNECTING

Maybe you haven't connected with someone in the past six months or a year. Lapses happen in relationships. But you are about to reach out and ask your network for help. If you have the time, reach out to those you have grown apart from, remind them of who you are, and let them know that you consider them part of a mutually beneficial relationship.

Here are two examples:

"Hi Nancy! It's been six months since I interned for you at Relativity, and I'm finally about to make the big move to L.A. I'm going to be sending out an email to my contacts soon to network for a job. I wanted to say hi and remind you that I'm the one who always wore the Red Sox hat and counted the pages before I distributed scripts to execs—LOL! Anyway, hope all is well with you. If there's anything you need that I can help you with, let me know. Jeff Hudson"

"Hi, Bob. I don't know if you remember me. We met at the PRSA mixer last summer when I was interning at Pro PR. I am graduating in a couple of weeks and moving back to Atlanta to begin my job hunt. I'm going to be reaching out to people for job leads. You seem very well-connected, and I'm a hard worker. I just need a foot in the door. Look for an email in about a month, after I've settled in. Thanks! Melissa Gretza"

It might seem odd to you to pre-email people to let them know you will be emailing them, but in this case, it will prime them to help you since you have taken the time to remind them who you are and give them a heads-up. In the first case, you've even invited Nancy to ask a favor of you. In the latter case, with Bob, you have also told him you think he is well-connected. Maybe he'll feel obligated to prove you right!

JOB HUNT PITCH EMAILS

This is a specific written version of the pitch you crafted in the last chapter of Phase Two, "Your Entertainment Career Pitch."

As with any version of your pitch, the job hunt pitch email should be:
- As short and to the point as possible
- Entertaining/reflective of your personality
- Forwardable without any editing

Using Jeff from the first example above, here's the email he might send:
"Hello everyone! I just graduated from Emerson and moved to L.A. As my mom keeps reminding me when she calls, now I need to find a job! I loved my internship in the story department at Relativity and ultimately I think I'd like to work in TV development, but for now, a foot-in-the-door job at a TV production company, network, studio, etc., would be great. My résumé is attached, along with a formal cover letter. If you know of anything, please let me know – and please forward my résumé to anyone who might have an opportunity for me. (I'm also interested in temping at TV-related organizations or working freelance on a show.) Thank you! Jeff Hudson"

And here's the email Melissa might send:
"Hi, all – As many of you know, I finished my Columbia College experience with a summer internship at Pro PR right here in Atlanta. Now I'm back to stay, and I'm reaching out because I am looking for a job. I want to work in PR, either at an agency or in the PR department within a local entertainment organization (production company, TV station, etc.). I'm a hard worker and take direction well. I have gotten very good feedback on my press releases, too! Attached is a cover letter and résumé. Please let me know if you know of any openings or if you know any PR execs who would be willing to grant me an informational interview. Thanks! Melissa"

The emails are similar, though in the first one, Jeff takes the opportunity to mention temping at the organizations he is targeting. You might wonder why you would be so specific when you have no job. What if there are temp opportunities at other companies outside your specifications?

Here's the deal: Unless you know them very well, the busy entertainment professionals you are sending this to will do only one thing – or, at most, two things – in response to your email. If you are specific, they will think specifically, sending the email to the HR department at their TV production company to have them add you to the temp pool, for instance. If you are not specific, they may forward your email to a friend at a real estate brokerage who mentioned at brunch the previous weekend that she needs someone to do computer research.

The more targeted and concise you are, the less effort the recipient has to make in order to help you move forward in your career. If you get 30 seconds of their time, you want them to be able to absorb and act on your email rather than put it aside to think about later.

TIMING YOUR EMAIL

The pitch email is a common entertainment job hunt tool. In most cases, you want to time the email when you can act on it. If you are moving to a new city and you want job leads, send the email when you are already in the new city and ready to interview and start working. If you send it before you move, people won't send you current openings they hear about because you're not available, and they will likely have forgotten about your arrival by the time do arrive. You can – and should – send the pre-email before you move, but hold off on the actual job hunt email.

 ACTION PROMPT 12

Create your Entertainment Network Tracking Sheet and pitch emails and reach out.

Note: As I said when you were creating your networking list, if you know Excel, I recommend using Excel spreadsheets for maximum flexibility. You can cut and paste information and sort columns, which will come in handy as the list grows and you need to keep track of information in a variety of ways. You will be adding other pages in this worksheet and grow it into an "Entertainment Career Home Base."

Step One: Create a layout for your Network Tracking Sheet that will allow you to keep track of the relevant information as you move forward and sort it as needed for different searches/uses.

Include fields for details such as job title, when you last had contact with them, what was said, referrals, any follow-up needed, and the date to follow up.

For instance, if Bob Smith, a VP at Lionsgate, offers to set you up with someone at Sony in a month when they are crewing up on a new TV show and might need a Production Assistant, you don't want to lose that information.

Below is a sample Network Tracking Sheet that is sorted by "follow-up date."

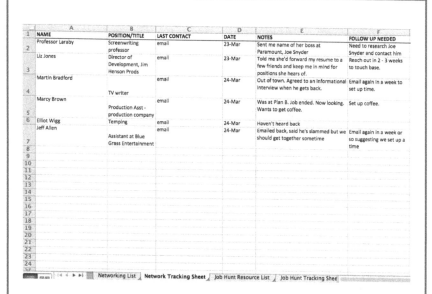

	A	B	C	D	E	F
1	NAME	POSITION/TITLE	LAST CONTACT	DATE	NOTES	FOLLOW UP NEEDED
2	Professor Laraby	Screenwriting professor	email	23-Mar	Sent me name of her boss at Paramount, Joe Snyder	Need to research Joe Snyder and contact him
3	Liz Jones	Director of Development, Jim Henson Prods	email	23-Mar	Told me she'd forward my resume to a few friends and keep me in mind for positions she hears of.	Reach out in 2 - 3 weeks to touch base.
4	Martin Bradford	TV writer	email	24-Mar	Out of town. Agreed to an informational interview when he gets back.	Email again in a week to set up time.
5	Marcy Brown	Production Asst - production company	email	24-Mar	Was at Plan B. Job ended. Now looking. Wants to get coffee.	Set up coffee.
6	Elliot Wigg	Temping	email	24-Mar	Haven't heard back	
7	Jeff Allen	Assistant at Blue Grass Entertainment	email	24-Mar	Emailed back, said he's slammed but we should get together sometime	Email again in a week or so suggesting we set up a time
8						
9						
10						
11						
12						
13						
14						
15						
16						
17						
18						
19						
20						
21						
22						
23						
24						

Networking List / Network Tracking Sheet / Job Hunt Resource List / Job Hunt Tracking Shee

Step Two: Copy the names and relevant information of people you are going to contact from your networking list to your tracking sheet.

Step Three: Note which ones need pre-emails and which will be in your job email blast. Categorize them as needed.

The people you will pre-email or will include on your email blast might fall into different categories:
1) Internship supervisors
2) Fellow interns
3) College classmates
4) Referrals from professors

You want to batch them this way to make it easier to email them.

Step Four: Create an email template for everyone and then customize it for each category of people you will be contacting individually.

In other words, you write a generic email that follows the following format:

What is the most basic way to identify you?
What job do you want?
How can you sell yourself for whatever your goal is?

Then take the basic email you write and polish it, taking into consideration which people you will be reaching out to with it. So your internship supervisors will get one version (and you might customize for each one depending upon how many there are and how well you got to know them), and your fellow interns, your college classmates, and referrals from professors will get their own slightly different versions.

Step Five: Send out the emails at the right time.
Reminder: Except for the pre-email emails, you should reach out regarding your job hunt at the time you can take advantage of any referrals or other leads you get. In other words, not more than a week or so before you will be in the place where your job hunt will be.

Step Six: Make note of all responses and future steps on your tracking sheet.
You may think you will remember every contract you make and everything you are supposed to do to follow up with them, but as you make more contacts and get further into your search (and then into your career), if you don't keep track formally, you run the risk of losing valuable opportunities. Trust me. If you make notes promptly in your tracking sheet whenever you connect with someone, you will not have to worry about missing out.

CHAPTER 15
FINDING JOB OPENINGS AND AN "IN"

In addition to working your network for leads on industry job openings, there are several other places you can look. Job posting sites, job posting aggregators, and company websites are some of them. But first you need to set up a place to organize your job hunt resources.

And as with compiling an entertainment network list and tracking sheet, organizing your job hunt resources may sound like a laborious process, but with the right system in place, it will take less time and be more effective than most entertainment job hunts. You're going to go through your job hunt resources every two or three days to find and respond to appropriate job leads before every recent grad in your area has sent in his or her résumé.

JOB HUNT RESOURCES LIST

If you used an Excel spreadsheet for your entertainment networking list and tracking sheet, just create another page for your job hunt resources list. Otherwise, an MS Word document will do. This list will include hotlinks to the sites you are going to search and will streamline your search. You will simply click on each one in turn every time you are taking a pass looking for openings, so this is not a list you can create offline.

JOB SITES FOR LEADS

Below is a list of general job sites and entertainment job sites, and a sampling of the job boards for specific entertainment companies. All of the major studios have outposts around the country, so do not ignore those sites if you live outside Los Angeles. They may have opportunities near you.

Two notes:
Except as indicated (*), none of the sites below charge job seekers. In general, you shouldn't have to pay to become a member of any site in order to look for job listings. Be especially wary of sites that imply they can actually get you a job in your chosen field and charge a fee.

Some job sites below are aggregators (**), which means they cull jobs from other sites rather than having employers pay to post jobs on their sites. There are a lot of aggregators that pull junk from everywhere. I have included only very good aggregators with quality jobs listed on them.

⭐ Search Engine
- Indeed.com (Enter your location and job specs, and it will pull up relevant job opportunities from many sites. Example – "Marketing Assistant" and "Austin, TX")**

⭐ General Job Posting Sites
- SimplyHired.com
- Monster.com

⭐ Entertainment-specific search sites
- EntertainmentCareers.net
- jobs.deadline.com ** (the job board of Deadline.com)
- linkedin.com/jobs (LinkedIn Jobs)
- Mandy.com (free registration required; premium version available)
- Mediabistro.com/joblistings/
- Media-match.com* (They have a free version and a $10/month premium version that allows you to create a profile and set up job alerts based on your search. It is worth the nominal amount for those features.)
- MyMusicJob.com (mostly internships, some paid positions)
- ProductionHub.com (free registration required)
- Showbizjobs.com
- Staffmeup.com (free registration required; low-cost premium option available)
- Unioncrews.com (for both union and non-union jobs – free registration required)
- VarietyMediaCareers.com

⭐ Company boards (just a small sample)
- us.blizzard.com/en-us/company/careers/ (Blizzard – gaming company)
- careers.discovery.com (Discovery Communications)
- careers.newscorp.com (News Corp, parent company of 20th Century Fox)
- sonymusic.com/page/careers (Sony Music)
- careers.timewarner.com (Time Warner)

- studiojobs.disney.go.com (Walt Disney Studios)
- warnerbroscareers.com (Warner Bros Studios)
- careers-umusic.com/umusic/jobboard (Universal Music Group)

KEYWORD SEARCHES

Another way to find job leads is to do a Google search for specific positions and locations, such as "Final Cut Editor job Madison, Wisconsin" or "Wardrobe Stylist job Washington, DC." Make sure to also do general searches, such as "entertainment jobs Washington, DC" or "television jobs Washington, DC" to make sure you don't miss any differently worded positions that are exactly what you are looking for.

SOCIAL MEDIA JOB HUNT RESOURCES

As discussed in the social media chapter in Phase Two, join Facebook and LinkedIn groups that are relevant to your career as well as groups for alumni of your college. (There may be specific groups for students and graduates from your program or only for graduates who now live in your area. Do some digging.)

There are also pages on Facebook where you can find jobs and on-camera opportunities, such as "Staff Me Up" for behind-the-scenes jobs and "Casting Notices" for on-camera opportunities. "Staff Me Up" also has Facebook pages for specific locations, such as "Staff Me Up Missouri" and "Staff Me Up Dallas."

There are Google and Yahoo forums for certain industries and alumni groups, but those are not as easily accessible. You will find them through your network and should definitely sign up for them if you get the opportunity.

OTHER RESOURCES

Cynopsis Classifieds – This is a job aggregator newsletter that comes weekly to your email inbox. It also includes expert advice on career topics. Subscribe through cynopsis.com.

The UTA Job list – A weekly list distributed by one of the top talent agencies in town, the UTA job list used to be an exclusive list of unpublished jobs. It was hard to get and was faxed, if you were lucky, or handed off to you or forwarded to your fax machine by others who were able to get their hands on it. That was then. With the advent of email and social media, it's much less exclusive and travels in a much wider circle. Less exclusivity means it's less valuable, but if you are able to get your hands on it, definitely use it to find leads. (Note: It's mainly but not entirely for positions in Los Angeles.)

Job listings on your local film board's site – There is a lot of money to be made by having a healthy production community. That is why some states offer out-of-state entities tax credits and other incentives for shooting locally. Most cities and states, and even some geographical areas (Southern Oregon, for instance) have film and TV boards (aka commissions) for the express purpose of connecting the producers of projects that could shoot in the area with resources, including crew personnel.

Independent websites that highlight entertainment opportunities in specific areas – I personally love hollywoodeastconnection.com. They cover information about the entertainment industry in New England and include a "Career Scene" section that includes job hunt resources, film board information, and other information about getting paid to work (behind or in front of the camera) in entertainment. Check it out even if you're not in New England.

ENTERTAINMENT PERSONNEL AGENCIES

These are, of course, geographically specific, so you're going to have to find your local area's temp agencies. A Google search for "entertainment personnel agency" and your town or area should turn up what you're looking for, assuming it exists in your area. Granted, there aren't many whole agencies specific to entertainment outside Los Angeles, but the areas with a healthy entertainment community will usually have a personnel agency that fill positions in entertainment organizations. (*More on finding out which companies use which agencies in the next chapter.*)

FINDING AN "IN"

What you really need when applying for a position in the highly competitive entertainment industry is someone inside the company who can refer or recommend you. If you can't think of anyone offhand and referring to your network list turns up no connections, it's time to visit LinkedIn.

You might remember earlier when I told you having a large LinkedIn network would help you with your job search? Here's why: When applying for jobs, you can use the search function to see if anyone in your network is connected to that company. For instance, let's say you are interested in a job at Ashton Kutcher's company, Katalyst. You select "company" as the type of search at the top of your LinkedIn home page. Enter "Katalyst" in the field. Search results will tell you if you have a connection who works there now (or used to work there), which would be a first-degree connection, or if one of your connections is connected to someone who works or worked at Katalyst, making them a second-degree connection.

Once you identify connections that are related to the company where you are applying, you can reach out and ask if they would mind passing on your résumé. That way, you don't have to just rely on the impersonal submission method provided on the job posting (though you should do that also, unless your "in" is someone you know well and it's a relatively small company). Depending upon how well you know your connection, he or she may even be able to put in a good word for you at the company where you want to work.

If LinkedIn turns up nothing, you can try to find an "in" through the groups and forums you are a member of. "Does anyone have a connection at Katalyst who I could submit a résumé through?" is a common question in these locations. Sometimes the requester gets lucky and sometimes even gets a job because of that "in."

JOB SUBMISSION TRACKING SHEETS

The job hunt resources list will help you look for openings to pursue, but you also need to keep track once you have applied for a job. This will be a record of what position you applied for at what company, how you found it, who you heard back from (and who you interviewed with, if you do get to interview for the job), and how you followed up. This will be helpful later during this search, if you find another job opening at the same company and want to reintroduce yourself, as well as for your next search and those beyond, when you see a next-step job posted at the same company.

TAKE THE TAKEAWAYS

Your head might be spinning after reading this chapter. There's a lot to know about finding and pursuing job opportunities, and you might be wondering when I will stop making you create spreadsheets. (Answer: Not yet! Sorry, but you'll thank me later.) As I said at the beginning, if you are organized, this will all become automatic and you will make quick work of finding that desired job in entertainment.

⭐ ACTION PROMPT 13 ⭐

Set yourself up for a streamlined job search.

Step One: Create your job hunt resources list.

Start with putting all of your resources (job boards, email newsletters, LinkedIn and Facebook groups, Google and Yahoo forums, personnel agencies, local entertainment websites, etc.) in your list. As I said above, you want hotlinks wherever possible, not just the names of the sites. Also include the names of job boards that you will either get emails from or that you need to log on to check, as well as newsletters you will receive and check.

	A	B	C
1	NAME	LINK	NOTES
2	LinkedIn's job board	linkedin.com/jobs	
3	Mandy	Mandy.com	
4	Media Bistro	Mediabistro.com/joblistings/	
5	Media Match	Media-match.com	
6	Production Hub	ProductionHub.com	
7	Showbiz Jobs	Showbizjobs.com	
8	Staff Me Up	Staffmeup.com	
9	Union Crews	Unioncrews.com	has non-union too
10	Variety's job board	VarietyMediaCareers.com	
11	Sony	sonymusic.com/page/careers	
12	Disney	studiojobs.disney.go.com	
13	College Alumni board	https://groups.google.com/forum/#!forum/bupride	
14	Cynopsis newsletter		comes every Monday
15	UTA job list		Jeff Allen offered to send
16			
17			
18			
19			
20			
21			
22			
23			
24			
25			
26			
27			
28			
29			
30			
31			
32			
33			

| ◄ ◄ ► ►| | Networking List | Network Tracking Sheet | **Job Hunt Resource List** | Job Hunt Tracking Shee |

Normal View   Ready

Step Two: Start your search and set up your job hunt tracking sheet.

The first time you go through your brand-new job hunt resources list's set of hotlinks and other places to look for jobs, let's hope you find a least a few that are promising.

To set up your job hunt tracking sheet (do I need to suggest using Excel again?), you will need fields for position, company name, location of job post, link to job post*, date posted, date found, date applied, reply, follow-up needed, date to follow up, and notes.

*Of course the link to the individual job post will disappear at some point. Until that time, it's good to be able to revisit it. And knowing when it disappears will give you an idea if the job has been filled, assuming you don't hear back.

	A	B	C	D	E	F	G	H	I	J
1	POSITION	COMPANY NAME	LOCATION OF JOB POST	LINK TO JOB POST	DATE POSTED	DATE APPLIED	REPLY	FOLLOW UP NEEDED	DATE TO FOLLOW UP	NOTES
2	Production Asst	Bad Robot	UTA Joblist	N/A	4-Apr	5-Apr	Email saying they got my resume and would contact me if they wanted to set up an interview	?	?	I think Marcy Brown knows someone there. Check.
3	Production Asst	It's Always Sunny	Media Match	http://www.media-match.com/usa/current/prodasst-job-25118700	5-Apr	5-Apr	nothing	?	?	Post on alumni board to see if I can find connection
4	Receptionist	Sony Music	Sony Music job board	https://jobs-sonymusic.icims.com/jobs/3024/receptionist/job	5-Apr	5-Apr	Heather Blaine called to set up interview on Monday	confirm interview date/time	8-Apr	research company & do other interview prep
5										
6										
7										
8										
9										
10										
11										
12										
13										
14										
15										
16										
17										
18										
19										
20										

Network Tracking Sheet | Job Hunt Resource List | Job Hunt Tracking Sheet | +

CHAPTER 16
GETTING A JOB WHEN THERE IS NO OPENING POSTED

As your mother and anyone else concerned for your livelihood will tell you, it's sometimes hard to get a job in the entertainment industry. However, it's not impossible. Sometimes, you need to get crafty rather than waiting to be the exact right person at the *exact* right time with the exact right qualifications for the posted job opening. That's right: CRAFTY. As in finding a job when there is no job posting. And sometimes finding a job where there is no job – until your résumé and cover letter land on their desk. Seriously.

TARGETING SPECIFIC COMPANIES

Just as Jimmy Fallon always knew he wanted to be on *Saturday Night Live*, you may have a place you have always envisioned yourself working at. Or even a type of place – a talent agency or a studio-based film production company, a record label or a reality TV production, for instance. And you know what? Those companies hire people all the time. You might as well be one of them. But how can you land that job if the companies don't even know about you?

At this point, you might think I am going to tell you to go ahead send your résumé to the Human Resources Department at those companies, along with an effusive cover letter about how much you admire the company because of A, B, and C – but I'm not. That's a rookie mistake that rarely results in a job. I've got a smarter way to go.

You are going to contact the companies you want to work for and ask them a few simple questions about how they hire, which will help you find and submit yourself for appropriate opportunities at those companies.

INSIDER INFORMATION AND READING BETWEEN THE LINES

Though you may not know the names of industry players yet, reading entertainment business websites, the business page of your local newspaper, the "update" section of your film board's website, and any other periodicals or sites that cover happenings in the entertainment community in your area can yield you some job hunt intelligence that might give you the edge over some less savvy seekers.

For instance, as I mentioned in the Job Hunt Resources chapter, HollywoodEast-Connection.com provides updates on projects coming to New England. If you want to work in production, this type of information is particularly vital. Movies and TV shows shooting outside Los Angeles always hire locals for the lower-level crew positions. These are usually highly competitive gigs to land, so if you can find a way to get the scoop as early as possible and submit yourself before the world is beating a path to the project's Production Coordinator, you have an advantage.

Other than production information, you're looking for local companies opening up new divisions, getting more capital, winning a new contract, or starting a new project. Also, you want to know if there are executives leaving or entering a company. In short, anything that signals change or growth is YOUR signal to use the instructions in the "Target Specific Companies" Action Prompt below to get yourself in the mix for new openings.

INFORMATIONAL INTERVIEWS AS NETWORKING OPPORTUNITIES

In Phase One, when you were career planning, I recommended getting first-hand resources for information on specific career paths. Now that you are job hunting, informational interviews can be even more valuable. You are seeing what is out there jobwise and getting smarter overall about the professional lay of the land. You probably have even more questions than you did when you were completely on the outside.

But also, if you can't find a posted opening for your desired entertainment industry job, these informational interviews can provide expert intelligence about where the opportunities might be, and even leads on, and/or referrals for, specific job openings. However, you need to tread lightly so as to not make the informational interviewee feel that he or she is being ambushed with an obligation to help you find a job.

TEMPING

This won't be for everyone, especially those who have a full-time job, but temping (doing short-term contract work filling in when permanent employees are out sick or on vacation, or doing special projects) is a great way to network and become familiar to entertainment organizations. You can to learn from the inside who does what and what you might or might not want to do for a living.

If you do not currently have a full-time weekday job, try to get set up with temp agencies that fill vacancies at some of the entertainment companies you might want to work at. For instance, if you are in law school but are taking classes only at night, temping for law firms that do entertainment work would be a great strategy.

WAYS TO WORK FOR FREE

As I mentioned in the introduction to this book, I started my entertainment career in Minneapolis. When I moved there, I had no master plan for my entertainment career (or any plan at all, really), but I was lucky enough to land in a small community of people, which included members of the Twin Cities film industry. And I was *thrilled* when I landed a Production Assistant position on a feature film shooting locally.

Well, some would call it an internship because I made no money, but I didn't even get college credit, so technically it was a volunteer position. But as I said, I was THRILLED to be an unpaid PA on an actual movie. I made some great contacts, including the Prop Master who hired me less than a year later to be her assistant on the next movie she did. I was paid $700 per week for that position, which was a *fortune* at my young age, so I relocated to Los Angeles for the job.

I must point out that much of this kind of unpaid work, though very popular and commonly called a "post-graduate internship," is not legal in California and may not be legal in Minnesota anymore (and for all I know, wasn't legal then). But while I am a *huuuuge* advocate of getting paid actual cash for your labor once you are out of school and in the so-called real world, sometimes payment is in the form of contacts and increased knowledge. Don't get abused, but recognize the value in taking select opportunities. If I could go back and do it over again, I wouldn't change a thing. When all else fails, working for free is the way to go.

Of course, some people have jobs or are otherwise unavailable for full-time unpaid work (and it is hard to come by, especially because of recent controversy and litigation), but you don't have to work for free in a full-time entertainment position to get valuable experience. Here are some types of things you can do for free that might launch (or supercharge) your entertainment career:

- Read scripts and provide analyses for independent producers or managers.
- Represent bands as their manager.
- Do social media PR.
- Do off-hours freelance editing assignments.
- Volunteer on student or indie movie shoots.
- Volunteer at industry events, such as film festivals, special screenings, conventions, or educational programs.

A day spent checking in participants and VIPS, giving out nametags, seating people, setting up supplies and equipment, and other low-stress activities can also be a day spent meeting and networking with entertainment professionals and other aspirants, picking up knowledge from the event, finding out what is going on in the entertainment industry in your area, and possibly getting leads on crew work and permanent job openings.

FORMAL TRAINING PROGRAMS

Getting paid to learn, develop your craft/career, and make contacts? Yes, it's possible. There are some formal training programs and fellowships you can take part in, if you are lucky enough to be chosen from the many applicants, which will give you a leg up in your career. Finding the right one is worth the time and effort. They are highly competitive, so if you are going to apply, make sure you treat the process as you would when you apply to any sought-after industry job.

ACTION PROMPT 14

Explore, identify, and try creative "in"s.

Part One: Create a targeted company list, call the companies on it, and do the appropriate follow-up.

Make a list of all the companies in your area that meet your criteria. It's called a targeted companies list. It will go nicely with your entertainment networking list and job hunt resources list. (People will see those lists and think, "Boy, are you on top of things!" And they're right – you are!)

After you have compiled the list, check to see if they have a job board on their website and then call the companies. Buddy up to the receptionist on the phone. Tell him or her that you're looking for job opportunities and you know they are busy, but you just have a couple of questions. You're using this introduction for two reasons: 1) To let them know you are not a representative of a personnel agency trying to drum up business; and 2) To let them know that you're not going to keep them on the phone long.

First, ask them how they hire temporary and permanent employees. Do they use a personnel agency, post on job boards besides their own, or use referrals? Usually it's a combination. If they say they use personnel agencies and post on outside job boards, ask them which agencies and which job boards. Write down everything they tell you in detail and then ask if they are hiring for any administrative positions now. That should be your last question. The other information is more valuable over the long term. If they say no to the hiring question and have to get off the phone for some reason, you will not get the information you have called for.

If they say they are not currently hiring, then and only then can you ask who you would address a cover letter to if you wanted to submit your résumé to keep on file. If they give you an email address, you'll send it both electronically and via snail mail. Unsolicited email is easier to delete or forget about than unsolicited snail mail – the latter can just sit on a hiring manager's desk until they get the brilliant idea (!) that you'd be a perfect person to consider for the upcoming floater position they need to fill.

If the person who answers the phone doesn't know the answers to your questions, ask to speak with someone who does. You might get a voice mailbox. Don't hang up. Ask the questions and leave your return phone number and email address. You will likely get a reply from this type of call. Very few company representatives will mind giving you the answers to the questions you are asking.

Add the job boards that company uses to your job hunt resources list and make it a point to sign up with the personnel agencies they use. Also, customize and send your cover letter and résumé to the company directly. If you've gotten a name to address it to (and with any luck, you have), call them about a week later to confirm that they received it. If they are curt with you, just be as polite as possible. Sometimes curt can turn into courteous. If they say they don't have any jobs, just tell them, "That's okay. I spoke with your receptionist, Jill, and she said it would be okay to send my materials in case something comes up." Smile while you say it. That smile will come across in the tone of your voice. It might also calm any nervousness you are experiencing.

Use this method with as many companies as possible. When an appropriate job comes up, submit yourself in whatever way they request and mention in your cover letter that you have been interested in working for the company for a while and had, in fact, submitted your materials and spoken with (NAME OF PERSON) to follow up. And then also send a letter and another copy of your résumé directly to that person, mentioning in the letter your eagerness to work for the company and your previous submission and message or conversation, as well as reiterating specifics on why you would be a good match for the posted job.

You may think this is too pushy or too much work, but it's not. You need to do whatever you can to distinguish yourself from the pile. And honestly, if I'm hiring and I have a million submissions, the person who does the most work to get noticed will probably get called in. Hard work as a job seeker usually translates to hard work as an employee.

Part Two: Get the inside scoop.
Add the names and links to industry websites (Deadline.com, TheWrap.com,

Variety.com, StudioSystemNews.com, and HollywoodReporter.com), your local newspaper's business section, the "update" section of your film board's website, and any other relevant sites your research turns up to your job hunt resources list. When you are going through the links, look for information you can act on. As I mentioned above, changes at the executive level, new projects, and new divisions mean potential opportunities for you.

Part Three: Line up and have some informational interviews.

Identify people who are doing what you want to do at slightly above your level, people who could hire you, or others in the same area of the industry who could provide more general information on how things work, how to break in, how to move up once you are in, etc. Reach out to those people to secure a fifteen-to-twenty-minute in-person or phone meeting where you can ask specific, thoughtful questions about what they do and how you should go about getting to do what you want to do.

Here are some tips for securing and getting the most out of an informational interview:

If you have no personal connection to refer you to the person, try to set up the meeting with an assistant instead of asking to speak to the person you want to meet with. Say something like, "Hi, my name is Jorge Smith, and I'm a recent college grad interested in working in post-production. I'm calling to request a brief informational interview with (NAME OF BOSS) so I can ask her a few questions about her career path and what she currently does." There's a good chance you'll get an appointment set up without further ado.

You may be asked what your questions are or even be connected to the person you are requesting an interview with right then, so it's important to have done your homework before you call. If they try to have the informational interview on the phone and you are in the same local area as them, ask if you can set a time to come in face-to-face. Say, "I would love to see your facility so I can get a sense of the environment. I promise I won't take more than fifteen or twenty minutes of your time." If they rebuff you or if you aren't in the same area as them, have the interview then. Better a phone interview than no interview, even though face-to-face is best.

For the in-person interview, dress nicely, show up on time, be prepared with questions about what they do and how you can get into that line of work, be yourself (the most cordial version of yourself, but relax, they are just people), and take only fifteen to twenty minutes of their time. Also, make sure to ask them if there's anything you could help them with. I know it sounds like a weird question if they're an established entertainment professional and you're a rookie. But you want to plant the seed that you could be of assistance to them. You never know where that could lead.

During or immediately after the meeting, write notes on what was discussed. If they offered to connect you with someone, asked you for help with anything, told you to check back in a specific amount of time, or anything else key that would involve follow-up, put that in your notes and by all means follow up in the requested manner.

Send them a thank-you email within the next forty-eight hours. Make reference to something you talked about, preferably something they told you that you found particularly valuable, and thank them for their time and expertise. If you can find something that is helpful to them (a good online article related to something you discussed or to their line of work, for instance), attach it. If they asked for your résumé, attach that, but if they didn't, don't. This is about expressing gratitude and doing requested follow-up.

A few days to one week later, if they hadn't requested your résumé, you can send it to them and ask for them to keep you in mind for anything they might hear about that would suit you. If you are looking for a job, reiterate the specific position you are interested in. If you would be willing to work part-time or work on a project for free, mention that, etc. This email may live in their pending file until they hear of the right thing, or it may be forwarded to a colleague, so you want it to contain all the pertinent information. This is basically a personalized version of your pitch email.

If one of their contacts comes through for you in some way or some piece of advice pays off, feel free to email them again and let them know how much you appreciate them taking the time to help you. It's always nice to get that kind of email. If nothing comes out of this relationship immediately, knock on another door and go back up to the top of this section and try again. (There is ALWAYS another door.)

Part Four: Look for temping opportunities, if appropriate, or ways to work for free

TEMPING – With any luck, when you did your targeted companies calling project (Part One of this Action Prompt), you found out what companies use which temp agencies. If not, call them now. Some companies don't use temp agencies, so you might get transferred to human resources to be put on the temp list. Regardless of whom you end up talking to, if you are actually looking for a permanent job, take a moment, once you establish rapport, to ask about current openings you might be right for. Though your main objective is to get that temp information, you may end up with an actual job opportunity.

WORKING FOR FREE – If you don't know how to find this type of work-for-free situation, look on your film and television board's website for upcoming events and other information, and post on Facebook and LinkedIn that you are looking for a particular type of experience. Work your network the same way you would for paid work. Once you are in these volunteer situations, remember that your goal is to meet people and show them what you can do. This is an industry that recognizes talent of all kinds, and people are always on the lookout for great help. So if you're going to take on the job of checking people in at a big entertainment event, be the best "checker-inner" you can be. You never know where it might lead.

Part Five: Research and apply to formal training programs or fellowships for what you want to do.

Below is a partial list of paid formal training programs and fellowships set up for aspiring writers, assistant directors, agents, and others that could help you get where you want to be in the industry. There are many others, so do further research on others related to your area of interest.

CBS Diversity Programs

diversity.cbscorporation.com/page.php?id=16
In a nutshell: A group of programs designed to provide career development and relationship-building opportunities to diverse participants in writing, directing, and acting.

Directors Guild of America Assistant Director Training Program

www.dgatrainingprogram.org

In a nutshell: A program designed to provide opportunities for a limited number of individuals to become assistant directors in film, television, and commercial production.

Disney/ABC Television Group Talent Development Program

www.abctalentdevelopment.com

In a nutshell: A program that identifies and develops diverse*, talented individuals in writing, directing, acting, or production.

NBCUniversal Page Program

www.nbcunicareers.com/page-program

In a nutshell: An more than eighty-year-old program established to give recent graduates exposure to the entertainment work environment through giving NBC facility tours and helping with tapings of live TV shows. (Approximately 75% of pages are placed in positions within NBCUniversal organizations when they complete the page program.)

The Nicholl Fellowship

www.oscars.org/awards/nicholl

In a nutshell: A screenwriting competition established to identify and encourage talented new screenwriters.

The Nickelodeon Artist Program

www.nickartist.com

In a nutshell: A program designed to nurture the development of emerging and diverse* artists for positions within the Nickelodeon Animation Studio.

The Nickelodeon Writing Program

www.nickwriting.com

In a nutshell: A program designed to attract, develop, and staff writers with diverse* backgrounds and experiences on Nickelodeon Network productions.

United Talent Agent Training Program
www.unitedtalent.com/#training/
In a nutshell: The agency's formal entry-level training program for mailroom personnel and other support staff to learn agency business practices and develop their careers. (Sometimes leads to promotion to agency status, but regardless, a top agency mailroom training program is impressive to have on a résumé.)

Universal Pictures' Emerging Writers Fellowship
www.nbcunicareers.com/universal-pictures%E2%80%99-emerging-writers-fellowship
In a nutshell: A program designed to identify talented writers and help them hone their talent by working on Universal projects.

Warner Bros Television Writers Workshop
writersworkshop.warnerbros.com/
In a nutshell: A highly competitive writing program for up to ten new writers per year looking to start and further their career in the world of television.

*When the organization mentions diversity, it is usually referring to people of color, but sometimes also older people or even women. It's worth a try to apply even if you don't fit into one of those categories.

CHAPTER 17
INTERVIEWS AND AFTER

A lot of people dread job interviews. They get nervous, sometimes to the point of feeling ill. But the job interview is actually a great opportunity. First of all, we (hiring executives, recruiters, potential bosses) already liked you enough from your résumé and cover letter to want to bring you in. If you are pleasant and sincere and somewhat interesting, meeting you could be the highlight of our day. And if you keep in mind that most hiring professionals are looking for the right match for the position, not the person with the most awesome credentials, you won't feel as pressured to appear superhuman. It's like a first date, without the potential for a goodbye kiss.

The guidance in this chapter is based on the hundreds of entertainment job interviews I have conducted, as well as the experiences of my colleagues, and those I've advised and helped prepare for interviews – what works, what doesn't work, and what seems to not work (you don't get the job you interview for) but actually works out quite well (you are hired or referred for a better opportunity). If that doesn't put you at ease for your future interviews, nothing will.

PREPARATION

Of course when you walk in, you need to know about the company. What does the company do? How did the company start, and what are its plans for the future? Who are the key executives? How does the company see itself, and how is it presented in the industry? Google the company's name and the name of the person you are interviewing with and see what comes up. (Ah, the Internet… Makes doing research so easy.)

Figure out what the dress code is and dress slightly better than it. If you can't find anyone who's been to the company (or, if the interview was set up through an agency, ask the personnel agent), you can use this as a guideline: Agencies, entertainment law firms, and the business-related departments of studios and networks (legal, finance) tend to be the dressiest. Wear a suit if you are male and the dressiest work clothes you have if you are female. For everywhere else, business casual is the norm: Khakis or slacks and a button-down shirt for men and the equivalent for women.

If you don't know where the interview is, drive there the night before if you can or leave a ridiculous amount of time to get there on the day of the interview. Even if you have been there before and know where you are going, allow plenty of time. The day of your interview is always the day they close the freeway. It's some kind of law of the universe. There is nothing worse than sweating out whether you are going to get there on time. It can throw you off and add to your nervousness – and, if you do end up actually being very late, cost you the interview.

Several days before the interview, review the job posting and think about your best related qualifications. It doesn't matter if you have already included those in your cover letter or if they are on the résumé. You want to stick to two or three key experiences or skills you have that make you a great candidate for the job. In political campaigns, these are "talking points" and they relate to why you should elect someone for the office he or she is running for.

In your case, focus on how selecting you for this job will benefit the boss, the department, and the company. For instance, if you are being considered for a Production Assistant job and one of the qualifications is being resourceful, come up with a story about being resourceful in another position, or in school. If you had to take over at the last minute for an ill classmate who wasn't able to complete her part of a group project, one of your talking points should be about how you got what you needed to do done in a ridiculously short time. This will show that you understand what might be asked of you and that you are capable and prepared to do what is necessary.

You also want to prepare questions about the job that you will ask if they are not answered during the interview. After all, it's a two-way street. What do you need to know in order to make a decision about wanting the job? Here are some questions you should consider asking:

Can you give me an idea of what a typical day in this job would be? If you haven't gotten a complete sense of the job, this is a good one to flesh out the description.

Why did the previous person leave the job? This is one of the two most important questions to ask, ones which will determine if you really want the job. Did they move up? Get fired? Quit? You may not learn much from the answer to the question, unless it's a positive story. "Oh, they're being promoted to Marketing Coordinator," the hiring executive might tell you. Good sign.

Once someone has established and proven himself or herself, how much room is there for growth? This is a more general version of the above question. In many cases, when you ask this question, they will give you examples of people who have been promoted within the company. If they dismissively say they want someone who is really committed to the job they are hiring for, that's not necessarily a bad sign. Reassure them that you want the job but also want to get an idea of opportunities beyond it.

What is the salary for this position? Are there benefits with this job? Is there overtime, and is it paid? I know salary is often the first thing on your mind, especially when struggling to make ends meet at the beginning of your career, but try not to make this the first question. And if you already know about the salary, make sure to find out about benefits and overtime. Benefits and overtime are important when considering whether you actually want a job. You may be on your parents' insurance now, but when you stop being eligible, having health insurance through your job is worth thousands of dollars a year. And working hours of unpaid overtime is something you need to be aware of.

THE INTERVIEW

Wait until about ten minutes before the interview to go into the lobby. For me, ten minutes early is exactly on time. (Look at that – I'm already impressed with you.) Assume the receptionist and everyone else who works there is assessing you for the job and will report to the people doing the hiring. Don't slump, complain about the parking, gab on your cell phone, ask for coffee, etc. You are interviewing from the moment you arrive at the office.

Bring three extra copies of your résumé. You will almost certainly not need them, but if the interviewer decides to have you meet with other people at the company and you save them the trouble of printing out extra copies, you have scored a few points.

IN THE ROOM

Smile, make eye contact, be pleasant. The interviewer is a person. Repeat: The interviewer is a person. If they ask you about yourself, it's not a trick question. They're trying to get a sense of your personality. Show them your personality. They will not hire you if they think you are a robot.

Say something that lets the interviewer know you did your homework. Even if you work it into a joke: "I read on Deadline that the company just got a new $500 million line of credit. Do you see any of that money?" Or comment on a poster from the company's first hit TV series. It doesn't have to be an analysis of the company's financial structure to get the point across that you know where you are.

Have a good reason for wanting the job. Don't say that it's because you live right down the street. I know that's sometimes an honest answer on our over-crowded planet, but let's hope it's not your number-one answer. Regardless, come up with something better.

Sell yourself. Use the talking points you prepared. If you don't have any directly related experience, use the experience you do have to demonstrate your diligence, your tenacity, your get-it-done-or-die-trying-ness. Don't be arrogant, but do let them know why you are right for the job.

After they have asked their questions of you, it should be your turn. They may ask if you have any questions. If they don't, ask if you can ask questions. Most likely the answer will be yes. If they don't let you ask any questions, it might be that they have decided that you are not right for the job, or it could mean they are just busy. If it's the latter, you should ask your questions either during the second interview or, if you get an offer after this interview, before you accept the job. You should know what you are committing to before you actually commit. Make it clear you want the job. Assuming near the end of the interview you still feel the job is a great fit, say the words, "I really want this position, and I know I could do a great job." This may not make a difference if another candidate is clearly a better match for the position, but in the event of a tie, I will go with the person who has expressed the most enthusiasm and confidence.

FOLLOW UP

I can't tell you how many people go from being a top contender to off my radar by failing to follow up after the interview. If you don't think to follow up, I will assume you don't want the job after all. (And even if you don't want the job, you should STILL follow up. You are not just looking for a job; you are building a career.)

Send a snail mail thank-you card immediately after the interview. If you have it stamped and addressed before the interview, all you have to do is write it and drop it in a mailbox on your way home. That way, it lands on their desk within a day or two.

Also send an email thank you at some point within the following twenty-four hours. Send it as soon as possible if you really want the job and are under the impression they are going to decide imminently. Your email should reiterate how much you want the job, mention something you talked about during the interview, and thank them for their time and consideration.

Don't panic if you don't get the job. You will have a long career, and an un-gotten job is just a blip. The relationship with the interviewer could be fruitful after all. Send an email saying, "Please keep me in mind if the candidate you chose doesn't work out or if something else comes up that you think might be right for me. I would still love the opportunity to join your organization."

I have personally hired many people who were not selected for the job they came in to interview for. Sometimes, I don't think they are quite right for that job so I "save" them for another opening I can't talk about at the time but that I know is coming up. Sometimes, I don't have a position for them, but I forward their résumé to someone else for a position at their company. You never know. You just have to do your best and be gracious in every situation.

DEALING WITH A JOB OFFER

For a first job in the entertainment industry, the considerations are pretty basic. If you have another job outside the industry that is paying you a decent salary, you can afford to be pickier than if you are just coming out of college or are between jobs in another industry. If you like your decent-paying job outside the industry, you can afford to be even pickier.

But at some point, you're going to have to think about your larger goals. Let's hope that during the first phase of this guide, "Entertainment Career Strategy," you did enough work to figure out what's most important or advantageous to you in terms of employment. If not, go back and revisit Phase One, Chapter 2, "The 'What,' the 'Why,' and Practical Considerations" for clarification.

TO NEGOTIATE OR NOT TO NEGOTIATE

If this is an entry-level job, there probably isn't a lot of room for negotiation. But you should negotiate anyway if:

1) You can't afford to live on what they are offering.

2) You have some related experience, even in an internship, and you know the offer they are giving you is at the lower end of the range they are hiring people at.

3) You want the job but it isn't worth taking at the rate you are being offered.

Be upfront and gracious regardless of the reason you are asking. Even if there is room for a higher rate, if you are rude in the negotiation, you could blow the job. That said, if you approach it with a respectful, positive tone, you aren't risking the offer. Start with something like, "That's lower than I anticipated. Is there any wiggle room? I ask because I really want the job but..." and then:

1) "I just can't afford to live on that salary." You could mention student loans, if that is the case, but if it is truly a low salary, you don't need to. They will understand.

2) "With my desk experience while interning at Sony and the temping I have done since graduation, I could be utilized in more than just an entry-level receptionist capacity." Whatever it is, be specific and focus on how you can help them.

3) "I just can't take the job for the salary being offered." If at all possible, incorporate something that will make them value you more, such as in #2. For instance, if the opportunity is within a company that sells a product or service and you have connections who would be potential customers or clients, definitely spell that out.

You may or may not get a counteroffer. Even if you decide to walk away, be gracious and leave the door open for a higher-paying opportunity, even down the road in your career. You never know what might present itself during your second or third or fourth job hunt.

ACTION PROMPT 15

Ace the interview and the follow-up.

Part One: Create a prep sheet for each job interview.

This prep sheet should consist of company research, talking points, and questions about the job. Yes, by "sheet" I mean that it should be written. Work on the talking points and questions about the job over the course of multiple days if you have the advance notice about the interview. You may think of more as you read over your earlier work. The writing process will help you internalize your thoughts about the job and why you might be the right person for it and what questions remain that will help you decide.

Part Two: Drive to the interview location in advance if you haven't been there before.

I know this seems like the kind of advice you'd roll your eyes at if your mom or dad gave it to you (and maybe you even rolled your eyes when you read it above), BUT if you want to work in showbiz, you can't be the one who shows up late for the interview. Especially in Los Angeles, traffic, roadwork, and parking issues are not good excuses; they're a GIVEN.

Part Three: Review your talking points and questions the day of the interview.

The idea is not to stick to the talking points or ask the questions robotically or repeat what you've written verbatim, but to have something in mind as you enter the interview that you can use to promote yourself for the job and show thoughtfulness about what might be important to know about the job. As I pointed out above, without something relevant to say, as a nervous interviewee, winging it can cause you to say something that does not promote you for the job, or even hurts your chances. Or it can leave you with to say nothing at all.

Part Three: Do your follow-up.

Send the email and snail mail thank-you notes. Even if you determined during the job interview that the position was not for you, you still want to cement that relationship by expressing gratitude for their time and for talking to you. You are building a career. Treat each person you meet as a lifelong friend. Make note of any suggestions they made, such as for résumé revisions or other places to consider submitting yourself for jobs, if this one doesn't work out. Also, make general notes about the interview. If you talked about something specific or learned something specific about them or their company that could come in handy later, write it down.

Part Four: Carefully assess a job offer.

Here are some basic considerations to help make the decision:

Does it pay me enough to live and/or enough to be worth it to me?*

Does it take me any closer to my current career goal (or support me in a way that is compatible with goals I will be pursuing outside of work)? Further, does it fit the parameters I set during the work I did in Phase One, "Entertainment Career Planning" (or make me rethink those parameters)?

Am I being considered for other jobs that I would want more?

*If the answer to this is "no" but you still want the job, see the above section on negotiation.

GETTING IN THE GAME CHECKLIST

Review of Phase Three

ACTION PROMPT 12

___ You created your Entertainment Network Tracking Sheet, preferably in Excel.

___ You copied the names and relevant information of people you are going to contact from your network list to your tracking sheet and categorized them.

___ You created your email template and customized an email for each category (or for each individual if you have a small network and the time to do so).

___ You sent the emails at the optimum time to help you with your job hunt.

___ You made note of each response and future steps on your tracking sheet.

ACTION PROMPT 13

___ You created your job hunt resources list.

___ You set up and used your job hunt tracking sheet as you found and started submitting yourself for appropriate opportunities.

ACTION PROMPT 14

___ You created a target company list, called the companies on it, and did the appropriate follow-up.

___ You created a list of industry websites and other resources to find insider information you can use to help in your job hunt and added them to your job hunt resources list.

___ You lined up and had some informational interviews.

___ You looked for temping opportunities, if appropriate, or ways to work for free.

___ You researched and applied to formal training programs or fellowships for what you want to do.

ACTION PROMPT 15

___ You created a prep sheet for each job interview.

___ You drove to each interview location in advance if you hadn't been there before.

___ You reviewed your talking points and questions the day of the interview.

___ You did your follow-up after each interview and carefully assessed each job offer that came in.

EPILOGUE
Your Entertainment Career

I want to congratulate you if you have followed and implemented even a sizable chunk (or, you go-getter, all) of the information and guidance found in this book. I know it's a lot, but I also know how overwhelming and intimidating it can be to be on the outside of an industry you want desperately to find your place in, whether you know what that place is or not.

My goal was for this to be a resource that could give you insider information on finding your way into this highly competitive and challenging industry. Forgive me if I erred on the side of too much information rather than risking giving you too little. I figured you would want all the help you can get. After all, they don't call it "breaking in" for nothing!

Maybe by the time you are reading this, you will have found that "first step" job. Maybe you will still be looking. Or maybe you won't have begun yet. But regardless, I want to leave you with a couple of words about the big picture. Yes, your first challenge is getting INTO the biz. It can take a while to get on the other side of the outside. The move from being *aspiring* (film studio employee, talent agency employee, wardrobe assistant, music management company employee…) to actual (film studio employee, talent agency employee, wardrobe assistant, music management company employee…) is a giant step forward. When it happens, you should celebrate.

And then what? How does someone go from Step One member of the entertainment industry to approaching and then achieving his or her ultimate dream goal, and have a long and successful career in entertainment? Take a lesson from these media moguls…

WHAT THE MOGULS KNOW

In Jay Z's book *Decoded*, he tells a story that perfectly illustrates what it takes to maintain an entertainment career. A magazine reporter asked him about U2's upcoming record. "I said something about the kind of pressure a band like that must be under just to meet their own standard," he explained.

After the article came out, he ran into U2 lead singer Bono at a restaurant they co-owned. Bono told him that reading that quote had gotten him a little anxious. In fact, "he decided to go back into the studio even though the album was already done and keep reworking it till he thought it was as good as it could possibly be."

This was not that long ago. Bono was already a rock icon. He had a twenty-plus-year career behind him. And yet even he felt the need to work a little harder to make sure he was still doing his best work.

Early in the life of Your Industry Insider, I wrote about paper mentors. These are people you probably don't know personally, but whose life stories (read about in articles and biographies) inspire you and help you make strategic moves and smart decisions in your career.

Starting in January 2010, Your Industry Insider has chosen a new member of the honorary board of directors each year, starting with the Chairman of the Board Richard Branson, followed by Jay Z in 2011, Ryan Seacrest in 2012, and Lady Gaga in 2013. Yes, that's right – Richard Branson, Jay Z, Ryan Seacrest, and Lady Gaga; four moguls with very different stories.

For Branson, the entrepreneurial spirit took hold at a young age. As a teenager he published an alternative student publication, which, at its peak, had a circulation of 100,000 readers throughout the U.K. He would go on to found Virgin Records, then Virgin Airlines, and then many more entities, now numbering more than 400 under his Virgin Group umbrella.

Jay Z was a pioneer in the world of rap music, starting as a performer then producing. Co-founding a record label and then a clothing line launched him as an entrepreneur. He co-owned a sports bar chain and part of the Nets basketball team, as well as an interest in many other enterprises.

Ryan Seacrest is a radio personality, television host, producer, brand representative, and beyond-budding media mogul. From his early start as a teenage intern at an Atlanta radio station that turned into a weekend overnight DJ gig, Seacrest has steadily added to his résumé, with no sign of stopping any time soon.

Lady Gaga, the newest mogul on the honorary board and the newest mogul in the real world, is a multiplatinum-selling artist, record producer, activist, and businesswoman whose endeavors include a fashion line and partnerships with retailers and electronics companies. She has also started to do a little acting, with cameos in a variety of movies. Though artistry and activism seem to be her central focus, hers is a steadily growing empire.

What do these moguls have in common? What patterns of thought and personal philosophies helped them get into the industry's "private jet set" and keep them on top? None of them came from especially privileged backgrounds. Jay Z came from the New York City projects, and Branson, Seacrest, and Gaga came from middle-class families in the U.K., the Atlanta suburbs, and New York City, respectively. But they all made bold, strategic, and expansive career moves, diversifying early, making key alliances, and not letting a lack of knowledge or related experience keep them from entering into new endeavors.

Rather than being discouraged, they took small steps into new waters. For instance, when Richard Branson got the idea for starting an airline, he picked up the phone and called Boeing to find out about leasing a jumbo jet. While in high school, Seacrest found a mentor who trained him in radio, and later dropped out of college to move out to L.A., where he landed hosting work almost immediately. When he couldn't get a record deal early in his career, Jay Z co-founded a record label, which spun off into a clothing line just four years later. Bold, strategic, and expansive? I think so.

Once you are in the industry, look around and see where opportunity lies. Where is there an opening; how can something be done better? Can you build a better airline like Richard Branson or found your own record label because nobody else sees your worth in the music marketplace? Can you l earn the ropes in your chosen field from a seasoned pro to cut out many years of trial-and-error and get to a new level quicker? Can you use your passion and artistry to expand your reach in the industry?

Hop over to Your Industry Insider to read all the lessons we learned from our board members, and then figure out how you can be the new Your Industry Insider mogul in 2025 – or even sooner!

CHAPTER 18
ENTERTAINMENT AS SECOND-ACT CAREER

Maybe you've been in the workforce for a while and you're doing pretty well – or even better than pretty well. But there's something nagging in you, an aspiration you left on the table because of laziness or loss of nerves or simply some other opportunity presenting itself. You always pictured yourself in the entertainment industry. That's where your passion lies, and you know "your people" are there, likeminded individuals with whom you could connect and collaborate.

But you're 29 or 34 or 47 or 53, and you're wondering... "Is it too late? Is it a terrible idea? Am I dreaming to think I still have time to start over?"

Well, it really depends. There are many examples of people for whom entertainment was a second career. On YourIndustryInsider.com, we have profiled a former teacher, apparel business owner, and even award-winning vintner, all now successful industry professionals. Your Industry Insider profile subject Page McCoy Smith, a longtime correspondent on WFAA's *Good Morning Texas*, gave up a job as a senior executive at a non-profit to become a TV personality.

Comedy icon Bob Newhart (*The Bob Newhart Show, Newhart, Elf*) was an accountant and then a copywriter before breaking into entertainment around age 30 when a friend gave Newhart's amateur recordings of fake phone calls to a record company representative, who signed Newhart to a record deal. Actor/commentator Ben Stein, a graduate of Yale Law School, practiced law, taught college as a professor, and worked in the Nixon and Ford administrations as a speechwriter. He did not start acting until his early forties, when he landed the role that made him famous, the droning economics teacher in *Ferris Bueller's Day Off*. Actor John Mahoney (*Say Anything, Frasier*) taught English and served as the editor of a medical journal before embarking on an entertainment career in his late thirties.

And contrary to what you might believe from watching reality TV competitions, the vast majority of people interested in getting into entertainment do not want to be performers – or even directors or screenwriters. Maybe you studied a subject related to your entertainment aspirations in college and maybe you didn't. Maybe you had a related internship and maybe you didn't. OR maybe you want to use what you *did* study, which isn't inherently related to the business, and merge the two.

Whether it is distribution or editing or representing talent as a manager or any one of thousands of other positions in the industry, most people just want to build a stable and successful career. Take that law degree and become a talent agent. Use that finance degree and all those years of consulting and start putting together movie investment packages or climbing the finance department ladder at a production company. Use "soft skills," such as networking and negotiation, to network and negotiate your way into the industry. A mid-career professional is *never* starting from scratch.

Of course, for established professionals from other fields who are considering a transition into entertainment, the big fear is that you let go of a good career and then don't get anywhere in your new field. Finding no decent job or discovering that you don't like what you *thought* you would like about the industry is worse when you've given up something that was pretty good, have a spouse or kids along for the ride, and/or you've relocated to L.A. to pursue your dreams.

The elements for making a successful mid-career transition into entertainment are the same as for someone just starting out. Financial, geographical, etc. factors come into play. But in the case of someone who is established and somewhat stable and satisfied in his or her current field, the considerations include:

Is this simply a reaction to being bored?

It happens. They don't call it a midlife crisis for nothing. Are you considering pursuing a dream that won't die or just trying to add spice to your life? If the latter, there are a lot easier ways to re-energize your professional life. Find a good career coach and explore your options before moving forward.

Is this something that is better as a hobby?

This is an interesting question, and it really depends on your goals and your situation. Of course writers can always write on the side and, until some steady money starts coming in, keep all sources of income in place.

If you always wanted to be a Broadway singer and you are a mom or dad in your mid-forties living in Denver, you should probably try getting into theater locally as a side pursuit and see where that takes you. Take some singing lessons to get your vocal chords back in shape and/or join an acting company. Put on a cabaret at a local nightclub. But don't quit your job or consider relocating unless there is some concrete opportunity somewhere else.

If you are a single marketing executive at a finance company with some money in the bank and you want to transition into entertainment marketing, that's an easier leap to make. If it's entertainment and not specifically L.A. you are aiming for, you might want to try pursuing a local entertainment marketing position rather than relocating to L.A.

What will I have to give up to make this work?

In the case of the marketing executive above, depending upon where you are on the corporate ladder, your geographical considerations (relocating or not), and the network you have (or not) in the entertainment industry, it could be a simple job change with a small step back or it could be a full transition, starting over from further down the ladder.

The bottom line for a mid-career move into entertainment is to make some low-risk moves first if you can in order to test the waters. Successful professionals often tout the benefits of "putting it all on the line," of "burning your bridges" as you try to achieve your dreams. But, as I said in an earlier chapter, it's easy to advocate that kind of all-or-nothing thinking if you're on the other side of making that leap. There's nothing wrong with some measured toe-dipping before diving into the pool.

That said, it's never too late to dip your toe in.

CHAPTER 19
BASICS FOR PURSUING DREAM JOBS

Success as a performer, director, or writer in the entertainment industry is dependent upon a combination of hard work, perseverance, smart moves, and more than a little luck.

Screenwriter/TV Writer-Producer Doug Jung (*Confidence, Dark Blue*), then solely a TV writer on lesser-known cable shows, attributes his big break to a bit of luck. After a general meeting (a meeting not related to pitching a specific project) with executives from Lionsgate Entertainment, one of the executives called a film agent at Endeavor, the agency that repped Doug at the time, to ask about a film script of Doug's that came up in the meeting. Since Doug was relatively new to the business and a TV writer, the film agent hadn't heard of him. But a production company executive was asking, so the film agent looked Doug up and went to his TV agent's office in search of the script.

As Doug relayed the story in his Your Industry Insider interview, when the film agent asked about the script, the TV agent took a moment to think about it, then reached under his desk and retrieved the script from a pile of unread scripts. (Remember, this guy was a TV agent. His job was to get Doug TV jobs. A film script was just another item on his to-do list.) When Lionsgate bought the script, that film agent ended up being Doug's agent. The script, *Confidence*, was fast-tracked to production and ended up being directed by James Foley and starred Ed Burns, Andy Garcia, and Dustin Hoffman.

Lucky though he might've been, the fact remains that most situations that are attributed to luck have behind them a lot of hard work and perseverance, and smart moves. In Doug's case, he'd gotten a day job as an assistant in the TV department of DreamWorks, written several spec TV scripts in order to have two that his boss at DreamWorks liked enough to help him get an agent, prepared endlessly for meetings about writing assignments and staff jobs, worked tirelessly on the writing assignments and in the TV staff writer jobs he landed, and then wrote and rewrote and rewrote *Confidence* until he felt it was ready to show his agent.

And only THEN did the stroke of luck come into play.

So while I can't teach luck, and I can't force a strong work ethic or the ability to persevere into you, I can give you some information about how the business works and some smart moves to make in order to be ready when that film agent comes down the hall looking for your script, or whatever version of luck you need to succeed.

LAUNCHING A CAREER AS AN ACTOR, HOST, VOICEOVER ARTIST, COMIC, OR SINGER-MUSICIAN

If you're really good at these pursuits, you make it look easy. An actor seems to effortlessly evoke laughter or tears from an audience. A host walks and talks with ease. A comic or singer-musician commands a stage. A voiceover artist makes us forget he or she is a professional. Behind all that effortlessness is years of developing skills, material, voices, instruments.

Picture the title character in *Rocky*, in the montage scene where he is training. He's jogging on an icy dawn. He's doing sit-ups. He's lifting weights. He's punching meat in a meat locker. Occasionally, he runs up the stairs of the Philadelphia Public Library and has a moment of inspiration, with the anthem "Gonna Fly Now" blaring in his head. But mainly he's just punching meat—for YEARS.

The actor performing in front of an acting class, the comic in the dank basement open-mic night, the host doing take after take for a no-budget web series, the voiceover artist repetitively practicing in her apartment, trying to get her tone right, trying to untangle a word that won't get past her tongue. Yep, the first step is…

STEP ONE: TRAINING

According to her interview on Your Industry Insider, the first question actress/voiceover artist Cat Campion asks when approached by aspiring voiceover artists is, "Who have you trained with?" "Nobody" is not an acceptable answer.

Actors – If you haven't already studied acting, in college or with private acting teachers (and actually, even if you have), find a reputable acting class to enroll in. Focus on honing and maintaining your skills, knowing that though the big-name acting teachers in Los Angeles, New York and regionally often have relationships with casting directors who come to them to find new talent, the key is doing good work. You have to audition to get into most classes. Unless you have a somewhat-developed audition piece, you most likely won't get into the classes that are competitive. And if you bomb, you ruin your opportunity to make a good first impression. So you should work to prove yourself from the very beginning. Walk in prepared. Be respectful. Earn your place.

For actors, part of the training (and maintaining your skills) involves being in student films and other no-budget projects, doing theater, and other unpaid acting work. Of course this is also a great way to be seen by people who could hire you for paid work, but the focus, especially when you are just starting your professional career, is to do great work.

Comics – There are two types of classes – ones for standup and ones for improv. Make sure you get into the type of class related to your aspirations – or do both!

For improv, The Groundlings, Second City, and Upright Citizens Brigade all offer training programs in Los Angeles, Chicago, New York, and other cities, in addition to having professional troupes. There is a competitive audition process to get into any of these, so you probably want to work your way up to them, and wait until you have material and comedic chops with which to audition. One way to develop your improv chops is to join a lesser-known troupe. In the major cities, there are plenty to choose from. If you don't find one you like, start your own.

For standup comics, part of the training involves getting up onstage during open-mic nights and trying out and developing material. When you are just starting out, you'll go up late, often when there are only a few (most likely drunk) people in the audience. You will bomb often, especially when you are starting out. It's expected. Don't let it discourage you. You will get better with practice.

Hosts – Find specific classes and workshops catering to aspiring hosts. Ask around, look online, and make sure you find one that is reputable and run by someone who has recent experience in non-fiction (reality or documentary) television, or other areas that use hosts.

Voiceover artists – The same advice applies to you. Find specific classes and workshops catering to aspiring voiceover artists. Make sure the teacher has professional experience in the field and is up-to-date on current trends in voice work.

Singers/Musicians – Training may or may not be formal for you. Some people pick up a guitar or start singing as teenagers and end up in a series of bands, one after the other, throughout their early lives. Rehearsing and performing regularly over the course of years is as good training as taking classes, though even if you don't have formal training, you usually end up studying the techniques of those who are more skilled, whether they are people you interact with personally or those whose recordings you study.

STEP TWO: TOOLS

Your performer résumé is usually just a list of credits with basic information included, with a headshot stapled on the back. Make sure your résumé is accurate and your headshot is current and of the best quality you can afford.

Your demo reel is a series of clips of you performing. If you don't know what to include, prioritize pieces where your individual performance is of the highest quality and, if you are an actor of the leading lady/leading man type, where you look your best. As performers, focus on material that shows you appearing in the type of projects you want to do in the future.

If you are a singer or musician, your reel should feature music you want to do more of, whether it's hard rock, hip hop, or commercial jingles. If you are a comic who wants to land corporate gigs, your reel should have your G- or PG-rated (i.e., cleanest) material. If you are an actor dying to be on a sitcom, select scenes that show how funny you are. (Note: These days, you can include clips you record yourself. As long as the production quality and content are good, there is no stigma with using "amateur" clips, though of course professional experience is better for your résumé.)

All performers eventually need a website. Don't go crazy. You just need a home base for people who want to see your résumé and reel. Even if you aren't ready to put one up yet, hop over to GoDaddy and reserve your domain name now. (If just your name isn't available, try your name plus "comic" or "actor;" something simple that will show up when your name is searched on the Internet.)

I recommend also having a newsletter or blog, and a Facebook page. And if you like Twitter, get a professional Twitter handle, too. (See Phase Two, Chapter 5 on your online presence for tips.) I know using this many platforms sounds like a lot of work, but it's not. These are just different ways to distribute the same or similar content in order to reach people who favor one method over another for staying up-to-date on their favorite performer.

STEP THREE: CONNECTING

Subscribe to the blogs and follow the Facebook pages (and Twitter feeds) of casting directors, agencies, and management companies you are interested in working with. Comment on their posts or ask questions in a way that gives them an idea of what you are up to. Example: "In my improv class at The Groundlings, they told us something similar. I'm glad my training there will help me in auditions!"

If you aren't actively shooting a project (such as appearing in a web series) that you can embed in your site, shoot one short video every other week or every month that provides a summary of what you've been up to. Whether it's taking classes, auditioning, shooting a digital short, or appearing in a friend's student film, you always want to have some ongoing items to report on.

Create written blurbs to let people know about upcoming appearances and disseminate them to all of your social media outlets. To save time, you can use HootSuite to schedule your blasts. Send a notice when you find out about the gig, airdate, run dates, etc. Send more notices as it gets closer. Send one the day before and/or day of, and afterward, thank everyone for coming/watching.

A FINAL NOTE

The people who are always "in action" are the ones representatives most want to work with. As an aspiring performer, you definitely need to be hustling as much as possible. Though everyone focuses on landing that big break and crossing the threshold from aspiring to actual paid actor/host/voiceover artist/comic, this type of self-marketing and promotioning yourself never stops. Having representation does not mean you just have to show up on the set and wait for the AD to come and get you from your trailer. It means you have help, but you still need to network, develop and maintain strong professional contacts, and promote to your loyal fans, friends, and family. Typically, the harder you work, the harder the other members of the team will work for you.

RECOMMENDING READING/VIEWING/LISTENING:

For Actors –
An Agent Tells All by Tony Martinez
How to Agent Your Agent by Nancy Rainford
Inside the Actor's Studio TV show on Bravo
The Business podcast on KCRW (Hosted by entertainment journalist Kim Masters, this show covers current events in entertainment, including interviews with prominent industry players.)

For Comics –
The Comic Toolbox by John Vorhaus
Comedian (A documentary follows Jerry Seinfeld as he goes through the process of putting together a new act from scratch.)
Marc Maron's WTF podcast (Comedian Maron interviews other comedians about their career paths and the life of a comedian.)

ON YOUR INDUSTRY INSIDER:
Actor Q&A with Director/Casting Director/Acting Coach Risa Bramon Garcia
Profile of actress/voiceover artist Catherine Campion
Profiles of working actors Nick Searcy (Justified), Josh Randall (Ed), and Kristen Vangsness (Criminal Minds)
Profile of Musician C.P. Roth
"Day Jobs: Paying the Bills While Pursuing Your Dreams"
"Three Great Day Jobs for Actors"
"Five Ways to Get a Leg Up as an Actor"
Pop Culture Lesson: "Things We Can Learn From Snoop Dogg and Kid Rock"
Pop Culture Lesson: "Things We Can Learn From Rob Lowe"
Pop Culture Lesson: "Things We Can Learn From Madonna"
Pop Culture Lesson: "Things We Can Learn From Mindy Kaling"

Launching a Career as a Writer or Director
As with the story of writer/producer Doug Jung's early years as a professional, behind every success is years of struggle. Behind every purchased screenplay, staff writing job, and paid assignment are reams of messy first drafts, problematic second drafts, so-so third drafts, okay fourth drafts, and so on. And behind every short or no-budget indie that makes a splash on the Internet or the festival

circuit, there are countless early efforts that didn't work for whatever reason. You don't hear about the years of struggle, the hours and hours spent by writers in front of the computer, slowly watching their blood (and sweat and tears) drip onto the keyboard as they type. And the countless be-your-own-crew film shoots that result in nothing usable. Not one frame of usable footage.

That's why they have to say you have to absolutely love it, or else find something else to do for a living. They aren't kidding. But you, you DO love it, right?

STEP ONE: TRAINING

The reams of bad first drafts and hours of unusable footage I just mentioned are your training to be a writer or director, respectively. By all means, read books about the technical aspects of writing and directing, as well as biographies of those who have been successful. And classes are helpful with the formats and techniques. But nothing (NOTHING) is more valuable than trial and error.

As you'll remember in the earlier chapter called "The Myth of Overnight Success," Malcolm Gladwell made a convincing case in his book Outliers that it takes about 10,000 hours of doing something to become really good at it. And I (let's hope convincingly) dispelled the myth of overnight success by giving examples of seeming rookies breaking through who actually had their 10,000 hours completed by very young ages. Writer Josh Schwartz and writer/director J.J. Abrams spent their youths studying and practicing their crafts, just as Steven Spielberg did.

So your training will consist of studying your craft, by taking classes and/or reading as much as you can, and practicing. Write. Shoot. Write more. Shoot more. It doesn't matter if it's good. Don't get too precious. It will get better. Think volume.

For the writers: Form a writer's group of the smartest, most motivated aspiring film and television writers you can. Meet once a month to critique each other's work, share challenges, and strategize next moves.

For the directors: Find a group of aspiring filmmakers you can create with. Be each other's crew. Find editors, costume designers, DPs, etc. though local schools, Craigslist, and/or social media. They all need material for their reels. It's a win-win for everyone.

STEP TWO: TOOLS

For writers, all you have in terms of tools is your work. If you're an aspiring screenwriter, you'll need one or two polished scripts in the same or similar genres, as well as some developed ideas when a potential rep or producers inevitably asks, "So what else do you have?" If you're an aspiring TV writer, potential reps and those who would staff you on a TV show have recently been more interested in original material than samples of other people's shows. One original pilot in the same genre you want to be hired to write in and one sample script for an existing show in that genre should be good calling cards for you.

For directors, your reel is going to be your main tool. It should have on it samples of your work in the format and genre you want to be hired in. If you are an aspiring sitcom director, make sure your reel is funny. If you want to direct horror movies, a horror short should be included.

STEP THREE: CONNECTING

For both writers and directors, the barriers to breaking through are giant, thick, steel-reinforced walls that can (and will) seem impenetrable at times. The only powers you truly have (and will continue to have throughout your career) are to create new content that you are proud of and to push it out into the world in whatever way you can.

For writers, once you have your polished samples and pitches ready to go, you should reach out to your network to get to industry contacts who might be helpful to your career. This will usually involve asking people to read your scripts. (Do a lot of favors for people because in most cases you will be asking a giant favor of them when you ask them to read your scripts.) The only people who will be potentially eager to read your scripts are the assistants to literary managers and agents, who can score points by presenting a promising client with strong material, and junior or new lit agents and literary managers who are seeking new clients for their roster.

Beyond your professional network, you'll want to go to pitch fests, writer's conferences, industry mixers, and other group functions where you will meet other writers and (more importantly) maybe some potential reps. If you meet someone and you aren't sure if he or she is legit, you'll have to use your instinct, ask around, and do Internet searches. There's a lot of "fake it till you make it" behavior going on in entertainment, so it's not a terrible thing if you ally yourself with a brand-spanking-new manager. If you have no other options, and they help you make progress in your career, it's win-win. But if anyone says they can get you an agent or manager if you pay them X amount of money, RUN. Getting a legitimate representative will always be on the basis of the quality and marketability of your work, your interpersonal skills (are you "good in a room," as the expression goes?), and a little or a lot of luck. You cannot buy a good agent or manager. Period.

For directors, you want to get your material seen by as many people as possible. Take it to the Internet. Have your own YouTube channel and promote it on social media and through email blasts. If you can build a following for your work, that will help when it comes to attracting representation or paid work.

In addition to your own material, offer to spend a day shooting footage, for free to prove yourself and get material on your reel, for others who might hire you in the future or for non-profits that can't pay you but do have a platform. It's great for your reel in both cases and for reaching potential clients in the latter case. It's even better if you can edit the material yourself. You never know where a day spent getting event footage for a publicist or a local animal rescue could lead.

A FINAL NOTE

In the case of both writers and directors, the name of the game is "make it real." Having examples of your work to show is the only way to get paid to create. Even many established writers continue to write their own spec (speculative) material (feature scripts and TV pilots) in order to move within the industry or simply to get something original out. Similar lessons apply for directors, especially since there's so much money riding on commercial shoots, features, or TV episodes. Create something great that you can show others, and you will make the powers that be feel that much more comfortable taking a chance on someone new.

RECOMMENDING VIEWING/LISTENING:

For Writers –
Bird by Bird by Anne Lamott
On Writing by Stephen King
It's Lucky You're Funny by Phil Rosenthal (memoir from the creator of Everybody Loves Raymond)

Writing the TV Drama Series by Pamela Douglas
And Here's the Kicker: Conversations with 20 Top Humor Writers on Their Craft by Mike Sacks
Beyond Screenwriting by Sterling Anderson

For Directors –
Rebels on the Backlot: Six Maverick Directors and How They Conquered the Studio System by Sharon Waxman
Rebel without a Crew: Or How a 23-Year-Old Filmmaker With $7,000 Became a Hollywood Player by Robert Rodriguez
Easy Riders, Raging Bulls by Peter Biskind
Down and Dirty Pictures: Miramax, Sundance, and the Rise of Independent Film by Peter Biskind
Making Movies by Sidney Lumet
Inside the Actors Studio TV show on Bravo
The Business podcast on KCRW (Hosted by entertainment journalist Kim Masters, this show covers current events in entertainment, including interviews with prominent industry players.)

ON YOUR INDUSTRY INSIDER:

Industry Pro: Writer Eric Rogers (Futurama, Brickleberry)
Industry Pro: Writer/Producer Doug Jung (Dark Blue, Big Love, Confidence)
Industry Pro: Writer/Producer Amanda Segel (Person of Interest, Nikita, The Good Wife, Without a Trace)
Industry Pro: Writer Alicia Kirk (Cold Case, Criminal Minds)
Industry Pro: Writer Stephen McFeely (The Life and Death of Peter Sellers, The Chronicles of Narnia: The Lion, The Witch and the Wardrobe, You Kill Me, Captain America: The First Avenger, Pain & Gain, Thor: The Dark World, Captain America: The Winter Soldier)
Industry Pro: Writer Christopher Markus (writing partner of Stephen McFeely – see above credits)